HINDUISM
A new approach

Veronica Voiels

Hodder & Stoughton

A MEMBER OF THE HODDER HEADLINE GROUP

Acknowledgements

The publishers would like to thank the following for their permission to reproduce copyright photographs in this book:

Philip Emmett 14, 17t, 26, 27t, 75 (both), 79t, 80b; NASA 39; David Rose 16, 17b, 19, 68t, 79b, 91, 101, 106; Mel Thompson 23, 25 (both), 28, 29 (both), 30 (all), 33, 35, 36, 41, 57b, 59; Veronica Voiels 5, 9, 27r, 27b, 57t, 68l, 71, 85, 86t, 89b, 90, 103. All the remaining photographs were supplied by William Holtby, John Smith, Bipinchandra J Mistry, Robyn Beeche and Ged Murray of CIRCA Photo Library.

The cover photograph, showing women tying bandans round a sacred tree, has been supplied by Robyn Beeche of CIRCA Photo Library.

Order queries: please contact Bookpoint Ltd, 39 Milton Park, Abingdon, Oxon OX14 4TD. Telephone: (44) 01235 400414, Fax: (44) 01235 400454. Lines are open from 9.00 - 6.00, Monday to Saturday, with a 24 hour message answering service. Email address: orders@bookpoint.co.uk

British Library Cataloguing in Publication Data
A catalogue record for this title is available from The British Library

ISBN 0 340 68350 3

First published 1998
Impression number   10 9 8 7 6 5 4 3 2 1
Year   2002 2001 2000 1999 1998

Printed in Great Britain for Hodder & Stoughton Educational, a division of Hodder Headline Plc, 338 Euston Road, London NW1 3BH by Cambus Litho, East Kilbride.

Contents

The author would like to thank colleagues and friends in India who provided valuable insights into the reality of Hinduism as a way of life: Professor Shubhada Joglekar from the S.N.D.T. Women's University of Bombay and her daughter Sarita, Professor Uberoi from the University of Delhi and Dr Ganapat Rege and Vikas who were so inspiring with their wisdom and generosity.

The author would also like to express her appreciation for the support and encouragement of Costel and Lucy.

Students' Introduction

This book will introduce you to some of the fundamental beliefs, practices and insights of Hinduism.

In doing this, it also aims to help you appreciate the value of differences in belief and outlook on life which exist in different cultures. It gives you the chance to become aware of your own responses to the moral, social and religious issues which arise, and to reflect on your own beliefs and values.

This photograph shows a Hindu priest who is a devotee of the god Shiva. He is surrounded by things that have great importance and profound symbolic meaning for him. What would it be like to be that priest? How does he see the world? Do you and he have anything in common? Do the things that surround him have a meaning that you can also appreciate?

As you discover more about Hinduism through this book, things which may at first seem strange will be explained and come to make sense from the Hindu point of view. By reflecting on them, you may decide whether or not they make sense from your point of view as well.

Teachers' Introduction

It is often said that Hinduism is a way of life rather than a religion. Thus the concept of religion needs to be reviewed and re-discovered in order to appreciate Hinduism.

For young people in the West who have been nurtured in a predominantly secular but nominally Christian society, Hinduism presents a real challenge, intellectually, emotionally and culturally. The usual assumptions that are made about religion do not easily apply to Hinduism and it presents students with a world view that is completely different from that with which they are both familiar and secure.

From a Hindu perspective, the universe has existed in many forms with many beginnings and endings, just as each living being may have had many previous lives and will have unknown future ones. God is seen both as an abstract force or life-giving energy, and as a personal deity in human form, close to the heart and dwelling in the home. Thus western students are invited to abandon their misconceptions, to become aware of their own prejudices, and to be prepared to be open to the possibilities of understanding this great religion, with its challenging notions which are often strange or contradictory to the western mind.

When these initial obstacles are overcome, it is possible for students to appreciate the unique qualities of Hinduism, its ancient origins, its rich visual imagery and mythology and its expression in social structures and relationships.

The value and importance of the moral and spiritual dimensions of life are vividly expressed and clearly understood in Hinduism, and it is hoped that by studying this religion students will acknowledge their importance too.

Since this book is written by a chief examiner in Hinduism at both GCSE and A Level, it aims to help students understand the key elements of Hinduism through its central beliefs and practices and to offer sufficient factual information to prepare them adequately for the current GCSE examinations in world religions.

It will also help students to understand and appreciate the effect of religious belief and practice on moral outlook, attitudes and behaviour, through guided questions and suggested activities.

But Religious Education also enables students to explore issues and questions which relate to their own experiences as young adults growing up in their own society. So this book consciously seeks to contribute to the students' moral and spiritual development by providing scope for further consideration of the content of Hinduism in relation to underlying issues about meaning and purpose of life. These are presented in the 'Think About It' sections and in the 'Question' boxes.

It is also essential for students at this stage to have an informed and sensitive understanding of the diversity of culture both in their own country and in the world, which can contribute to their development as citizens of the world.

So this text book reflects an approach to RE which emphasises the personal quest for meaning and values, as well as contributing to multi- cultural education.

1

Hinduism as a Way of Life

- Dharma
- The Origins of the Caste System
- The Four Stages of Life
- The Four Aims in Life

Anyone from the West who has travelled in India will comment on the crowded streets and chaotic traffic. There are often traffic jams in Varanasi when all the visitors arrive. Bullock carts, cycle rickshaws, auto rickshaws and taxis jostle with holy men, pilgrims and street vendors. All walks of life can be found together in this Indian street.

Hinduism is unique among all the religions of the world in several ways. First of all Hinduism is not a religion or dogma but a comprehensive co-operative complimentary and self re-vitalising way of life. Hinduism is the name given to this very old but ever young, vital and vibrant way of life.

Mathoor Krishnamurti

The notion that Hinduism is not a religion but more a way of life is sometimes difficult for people in western culture to understand because everyone has a way of life but not everyone has a religion. In the West, people sometimes separate religion (i.e. faith in and worship of God) from non-religious or secular areas of life, such as work and family life. Yet in Hinduism, the way of life of a Hindu is a religion in itself. In reality, a person's beliefs (whether religious or non-religious) affect their intentions, thoughts, attitudes and behaviour in every aspect of life. This is very clearly understood and appreciated in Hinduism.

Dharma

A central concept in understanding Hinduism as a way of life is **Dharma**. The origin of this Sanskrit word comes from *'Dhru'* which means to hold, to exist, to remain or to support. It relates to the concept of *Rta* in the ancient Vedic hymns, which refers to the cosmic order and law of the universe. Rta is the harmony and order which must be preserved and maintained to prevent the collapse and disintegration of all the worlds and every society. Thus Dharma refers to what is right and what is true, it applies to the laws governing the duties of people and also the laws governing the universe itself. It is often interpreted as 'religion'.

The concept of Dharma is linked to the law of **Karma** (the law of cause and effect). This claims that nothing happens by accident, but has been caused by some action in the immediate or distant past. So it is necessary for everyone to consider the future consequences of their thoughts and deeds since they will affect the future conditions and circumstances they find themselves in. So how does a person know what to do in order to ensure good consequences from their actions?

For Hindus, this means they must follow the laws and duties of dharma. They must act in accordance with dharma. These are the moral principles which will ensure a stable, harmonious and healthy society within which people can live.

These moral principles are expressed in two ways in Hinduism, firstly as **Sanatana Dharma** which means 'eternal law' and secondly **Varnashramadharma** which means 'the laws and duties for each caste and stage in life.'

> The word Hindu is derived from the word 'Sindhu', the name of the River Indus. The early Persians called that portion of the country bordering on the Indus River, Sindhu. The word was corrupted into Hindu and still further corrupted by the Greeks as 'Indoi' from which the word 'India' comes.

Although Hinduism originated in India, it has spread throughout the world. This map shows countries in which there are 10,000 or more Hindus.

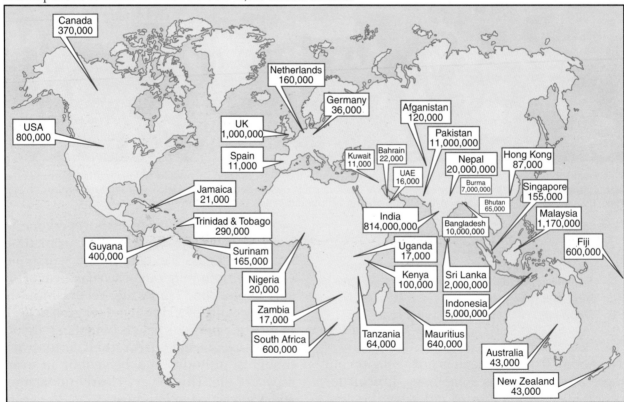

Sanatana Dharma

This means the eternal law or eternal religion. Matoor Krishnamurti, a spokesman for modern Hinduism, explains that Sanatana Dharma is the true name of Hinduism, and that Hindus are followers of this eternal and universal law.

Sanatana Dharma refers mainly to the principle of **Ahimsa** (non violence) and other principles such as **satya** (truth), **asteya** (not stealing), **sauca** (purity) and control of the senses. The practice of ahimsa has always been a distinctive feature of Hinduism and is expressed in a variety of ways:

> *'Having no ill feelings for any living being in all manners possible and for all times is called ahimsa.'*
> *'A teacher, a propounder of the scriptures, father mother, guru, brahmin, cow and ascetic: they should never be killed'*
>
> *(Manu-smriti 4.162)*

In India cows are allowed freedom to roam where they wish and are sometimes cared for by temple priests. They are considered to be sacred beasts, even deities, because of their ability to provide essential needs of life - nourishment of milk and cow dung for fuel.

Thus ahimsa is shown in regarding the cow as a sacred animal and the killing of it as a form of murder. Gandhi based his whole philosophy of life upon this principle and encouraged the practice of non-violence as a form of political protest in the movement for independence from British Rule.

Activities

Key Elements

1 Explain the following in your own words: Dharma; Sanatana Dharma; Karma.

2 Why is Ahimsa so important for Hindus, and how is it put into practice?

Think About It

3 How might the following beliefs affect a person's behaviour?

  (i)   Human beings are all basically good

  (ii) Human beings are all basically bad

  (iii) There is life after death

  (iv) This is the only life there is.

4 Is there any difference between a religious and a non-religious outlook on life? If so, what is it?

Varnashramadharma

In trying to understand what it means to be a Hindu and to follow the Hindu way of life, it is necessary to understand and appreciate the meaning of the concepts of **Varna** and **Ashrama**.

A Hindu's sense of identity is determined by the caste (varna) they are born into and the particular stage of life (ashrama) they are in.

So as well as the general principles of morality enshrined in dharma, there are very particular responsibilities and duties related to caste and stage in life.

> ## Question
>
> * What does Varnashramadharma mean? Explain it in terms of the three words that make it up.

Varna

This term is often translated as caste but it really refers to the four main social groupings which are the basic structure of Hindu society.

The idea of being born into a social grouping which can never change and which is hereditary is something which people in the West find difficult to appreciate, as it is possible to move out of one's social class if the opportunity comes along.

However, in Hinduism there are considered to be four main social groups:

* Brahmins
* Kshatriyas
* Vaishyas
* Shudras.

In simple terms these refer to the priestly class (brahmins), the warriors (kshatryas) the merchant classes (vaishas) and the servant classes (shudras)

These seem to have little relationship to the social classes which operate in modern society but they can be interpreted as follows:

The Brahmins are those charged with the responsibility for preserving the traditions and rituals of Hinduism, understanding and passing on the teachings of the scriptures and setting a good moral example to others by remaining pure in words and deeds. They are the priests and professional classes in society

This is a brahmin family, engaged in a religious ritual outside their home. They have made a special altar with offerings and are reading out loud from the sacred scriptures.

A brahmin priest at Tirupur. This man is identified as a priest of the brahmin caste because he is wearing a sacred thread (see page 94). The notion of purity and pollution is part of the Hindu understanding of caste. A brahmin is considered to be pure in body and mind, and therefore the best person to make offerings to the deities. In this picture the priest is simply wearing a dhoti, and has cleansed his body and then marked himself with the symbolic three white horizontal lines of a Shaivite devotee (someone who is particularly devoted to the god Shiva, see page 26). He is holding a tray of flowers which are to be used as offerings.

The Kshatriyas are those who have responsibility for leadership, ruling society, making decisions about the general welfare of the people, defending them from injustice and tyranny. They are the administrators and military forces in society.

The Vaishyas have responsibility for providing the material goods and the wealth of society. They are the business people in society

The Shudras have the responsibility for doing the physical and manual work and serving the needs of the other castes. They are the craft workers and servants in society.

Questions

- To what extent do you think your family background influences the choice of what you will do in life?

- In traditional Hindu society, you will have been born into a particular caste and that will influence many things in your life. Make a list of the advantages and disadvantages you see in having your life influenced in that way.

- If you could choose to be born into one of the four main Hindu castes, which would it be and why?

This man is a basket weaver. This is not just his occupation, but shows his place within the caste system. Baskets like this, which in the West are used mainly for decorative purposes, are essential for a whole variety of tasks in Indian village life.

The Origins of the Caste System

There are several theories about how the caste system came about:

The racial origins of caste

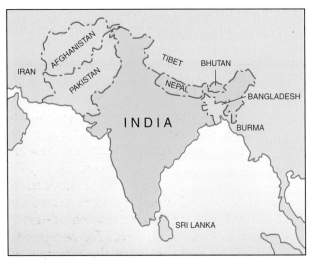

India in relation to the countries that surround it. Note the positions of Iran and Pakistan. The Aryans may have migrated from Iran or have been one of many tribes already living in northwest India.

When the Aryan peoples came to dominate the northern and western parts of India from about 1500 BCE, they introduced their way of life and social structure. Their brahmins were priests and poets who composed hymns to the gods and performed rituals to ensure the favour of the gods. The kshatriyas were the chieftains who established their authority over their own tribesmen and those who already lived in India.

As they became more settled, the Aryans engaged in trading and production of goods and needed an organised workforce. This could be how the vaishya and shudra castes developed.

The word varna comes from a Sanskrit word meaning colour and suggests that the caste system is related to the distinction between the fairer-skinned inhabitants of India whose ancestors may have been Aryans and the darker skinned inhabitants of India, the Dravidians whom the Aryans called Dasas or Dasyus.

Since the shudras may have been the original inhabitants of India described as dark-skinned peoples in the early hymns of the vedas, the varna system could be related to the superiority of the fair-skinned Aryans over the dark-skinned inhabitants who were absorbed into Aryan society but given a lower place within it.

A religious explanation of the origin of the varna system

The ancient Vedic scriptures contain a hymn which could be seen as an explanation for the caste system. The hymn presents the caste system as a division of the peoples of the world which was established at the beginning of time through the creative activity of the Supreme Being, Purusha, the primal man.

> *When they divided primal man*
> *Into how many parts did they divide him?*
> *What was his mouth? What his arms?*
> *What are his thighs called? What his feet?*
>
> *The Brahmin was his mouth,*
> *His arms were made the Prince,*
> *His thighs the common people*
> *And from his feet the shudra were born.*
>
> (Rig Veda X, xc: 11-12.
> Translated by R.C. Zaehner)

This hymn shows that:
- the priest's authority comes from the words he utters with his mouth when teaching and reciting the scriptures;
- the warrior's authority comes from his strength when defending the people from enemies;
- the merchants and farmers support these two classes, just as the thighs keep the body upright;
- and finally the shudras provide all the services to the three upper varnas.

Thus the brahmins are at the top of the social scale and the shudras at the bottom.

The division of the four social classes was not as rigid in these early times as it later became, and the law books of Manu, composed between 200 BCE and 200 CE, prescribe very detailed duties for each of the four varnas. In these law books the first three varnas are termed 'twice born' and they have a second spiritual birth when they receive the sacred thread, and can study the Vedas. The shudras do not receive the sacred thread and cannot study the Vedas.

The religious origin of caste has been differently interpreted in the Bhagavad Gita. Here, according to Matoor Krishnamurti, caste is determined by the character of a person not according to his or her birth.

> 'The works of a Brahmin are peace: self harmony, austerity and purity; loving forgiveness and righteousness; vision and wisdom and faith.
> These are the works of a Kshatriya; a heroic mind, inner fire, constancy, resourcefulness, courage in battle, generosity and noble leadership.
> Trade, agriculture and the rearing of cattle is the work of a vaishya. And the work of a Shudra is service.'

> (Bhagavad Gita Chapter 18 verses 42-44
> Translated by Juan Mascaro)

Together with this comes the belief that the social class a person is born into is the result of their previous actions or the law of karma. If their personality, temperament, actions and behaviour are developed in a pure and moral way then they are likely to take the form of a brahmin in the next existence and so forth. Thus the belief in karma reinforces the acceptance and purpose of the varna system.

The social origins of caste

Although the varna defines the four general social groupings, what is more important and relevant to Hindus, especially the 75% who live in villages, is their occupational status or job. This is known as **Jati** which is the more accurate translation of caste. As society developed from the earliest Vedic times, the variety of specialised occupations increased as each village or settlement required its potters, weavers, basket-makers, shoemakers, carpenters etc. Most jatis or castes refer to such traditional occupations and in the course of time they were passed on from father to son and so became hereditary.

Eventually these occupations formed guilds or associations and protected the interests of their members and became exclusive, rather like clubs in which only members of the same occupation were allowed to join. Then a hierarchy of jatis or castes developed in which rules forbidding marriage and dining between castes developed.

This man is a laundryman. It is his jati, or family occupation. He has an essential role to play in village life. He and his family will probably have been doing this kind of work for generations.

These social rules became more elaborate and fixed and form the basis of caste customs today. A Hindus caste status affects people's lives quite strongly in determining:

(i)   the kind of job they are trained in
(ii) the people they would eat with or share food with
(iii) the person they would marry.

In spite of many attempts to undermine the effects of caste it is deeply rooted in Hindu culture to marry within the same caste. The higher up the ladder the caste the greater their purity is and so to marry a person from a lower caste is considered to be very degrading.

There are many rules related to marriage and eating together based on caste distinctions.

In Hinduism, the notion of purity and pollution is associated with caste, the dirtier jobs are regarded as polluting by those who belong to the higher castes.

Because some tasks were considered to be particularly unclean, especially those dealing with dead animals or rubbish, the castes who performed them were thought to be so unclean as to be outside the caste system altogether. These people became known as the untouchables or Harijans.

Responses to caste in India and Britain today

Amongst Hindus today there are a variety of attitudes towards caste. In the more traditional way of life in the villages it is still quite a dominant factor, because it helps to provide security and stability by giving everyone an essential role and function to play to keep village life running smoothly. Most villages have a caste council which offers help and support to its members, rather like a social security system at grass roots level.

However, Indian society is changing and as India becomes a more developed, industrialised country, so traditional occupations are changing and new ones are developing. The result is that life in a modern urban environment makes it difficult, if not irrelevant, to observe caste customs.

This man is a cobbler. His work involves leather, and since contact with the skins of dead animals is particularly polluting, he is a Harijan. No Hindu from a higher caste would consider doing work of this sort.

What is more, discrimination on the grounds of caste is forbidden in the Indian constitution, and to ensure that they get a fair share of the benefits of education, special places are reserved for the lower castes and 'unscheduled castes' (another term used for people who are 'outcastes' or 'untouchables') in institutions of education.

There are countless examples of members of different varna or castes choosing not to follow traditional occupations. Some very able people from lower castes have achieved a great deal more than would have been expected of them when they were born.

One particularly famous man, who was a key member of the Indian Congress in its writing of the Indian constitution, was born an 'untouchable'. His name was Ambedkar. In spite of many difficulties, he went to universities both in India and in the United States, and became very well respected as a lawyer. He used his powerful position in the newly independent India to seek to improve the material well-being of the underprivileged classes, and his position gave encouragement to others who wanted to improve their lives.

He also ensured that 'untouchability' was outlawed by the Indian constitution.

Many other reformers in Hinduism in the nineteenth and twentieth centuries, such as Gandhi and Swami Vivekananda, also campaigned against the injustices of the caste system and 'untouchability'.

So, amongst Hindus today there are some who would like to see the caste system die out but that will not happen easily:

Old habits die hard. The hearts of the people must change which will only happen when the upper castes are prepared to change their attitudes and acknowledge the fluidity of caste in ancient times and the need for this to-day, as well as the inter-mixing of castes within each one of us.

Shakunthala Jagannathan (a modern Hindu writer who has travelled around the world promoting and explaining Indian culture.)

One of the areas where caste distinctions are particularly noticeable is in temple worship.

In India some temples are banned to those of lower castes. This is due to the notions of purity and impurity associated with upper and lower castes. In Britain today the issue of observing caste rules is often discussed amongst the local communities and temple councils. While most of their temples are open to all castes there are others who want the caste distinctions to remain.

For young Hindus who are born and brought up in Britain, the caste laws seem less important to them than the older generation whose outlook has been formed by their experiences in the villages and cities of India.

However, despite all the changes to Indian society in recent years, and the experience of Hindu communities in all parts of the world, the issue of caste remains one in which a variety of views and opinions still exist, and it continues to have a profound influence on the life of the Hindu community.

Discussion

- What is meant by a sense of identity?
- Where do you get your sense of identity from?
- How do the following contribute to your sense of identity: parents / friends / the place where you live / your social class?

Activities

Key Elements

1 What does the hymn on page 12 have to say about the origins of the caste system?

2 What are the duties of the Brahmin, Kshatriya, vaishya and shudra castes?

3 Is there any difference between jati and varna? If so, what is it?

Think About It

4 (a) Why do some people in the West think the caste system is unfair?

(b) What are the benefits of the caste system for village life in India?

(c) Which of the theories for the existence of the caste system do you find most convincing and why?

(d) Why is the caste system still a strong feature of the Hindu way of life?

The Four Stages of Life (The Ashramas)

Just as each caste has its particular duty to follow, there is also dharma for the four **ashramas** or stages in life. These stages follow the natural process of growing up and growing old in society, but also recognise the importance of duties to society and the need to attend to the spiritual aspects of life. The ancient Law Books of Manu describe these four stages of life.

Brahmacharyi or student

This begins with the initiation rite of the sacred thread (**upanayana**) which is performed only on the three upper varnas. In ancient times it was also performed on girls, as can be seen in temple sculpture, but this was given up later on.

In the past this stage would involve studying the Vedic scriptures under the guidance of a specially chosen guru or priest. It would also involve leaving the family home and living at the guru's special school (gurukula) traditionally in the forest or some secluded place.

It was a life which involved service to the guru and his family, the practice of yoga, the study of scriptures, the arts and sciences and a life of simplicity, celibacy and spartan self discipline.

On their departure after training, the guru exhorted his pupils to speak only the truth, never to forget dharma, to serve elders, to remember the teachings of the vedas and to regard one's mother, father, teacher and guest as divine beings, to be honoured and revered.

Nowadays very few boys attend these traditional schools to study the scriptures but attend the primary and secondary schools in their neighbourhood, but it is still regarded as a student's duty to gain knowledge by a course of study, to show regard for teachers and parents and to learn the rules and rituals of the Hindu tradition.

Grihasta or Householder

In the West, many people live in what is called a 'nuclear family' - mother, father and children living together. There are many single parent families and people who choose to live on their own. Hinduism, by contrast, places great importance on the extended family - relatives of three or even four generations living together. This family have gathered for a picnic in the fortress in Rajastan.

This stage begins when the student returns from his studies, marries and takes on the duties of a householder.

This stage is considered to be very important, as marriage is a sacred duty for Hindus in order to continue the family and all the social and religious obligations that go with it. The word vivaha (marriage) also means 'that which sustains dharma or righteousness'. No religious

A traditional gurukula.

ritual can be performed by a man without his wife, and no man or woman's life is seen as complete without marriage.

Householders are expected to:
- give to charity
- care for aged parents
- offer hospitality to guests
- provide a settled, well run household.

A married woman's duties include:
- bringing up the children
- managing the household expenses
- preparing food
- keeping the home clean
- organising the celebration of festivals and other religious rites.

Today many Hindu woman have full-time jobs as well.

A husband must:
- provide for his wife and children
- educate and arrange marriages for his sons and daughters
- earn money honestly
- spend it on ways which are beneficial to himself and others.

Religious rituals in a temple involve the whole family.

Discussion

- What do you think about the responsibilities of husbands and wives in traditional Hindu families? Would you want to change any of them? If so, why?

The photograph below shows a single extended family! One hundred and twenty seven family members have gathered to have their photo taken in front of the Taj Mahal.

Vanaprastha (retirement stage)

This stage occurs when the children are grown up and able to run their own lives and when the first son of the first son is born, so it is certain that the family will continue. The head of the household is then able to hand over his responsibilities to his eldest son.

Varnaprastha is the time of retirement from daily work. In ancient times this was marked by becoming a forest dweller, which is what vanaprastha really means, but today few people would actually go out to a forest.

The duties of this stage are:
- to become detached from worldly and material concerns
- to devote time to quietness and solitude
- to study the scriptures
- meditation.

Those in this stage are seen as wise elders in the family and are called upon for advice and help in educating the children. Not all Hindus take on the particular duties of this stage, but those who do are highly respected.

Sannyasin (renunciation stage)

This stage of life is especially respected in Hinduism. It involves:
- the complete giving up (renouncing) of all worldly ties and possessions
- devoting one's entire life to the spiritual goal of liberation (moksha).

Some sannyasins become wandering holy men with no fixed abode. They spend their whole life on pilgrimage, in prayer, meditation and study of the scriptures.

Not many Hindus enter this stage but it is regarded very highly as a holy and spiritual way of life.

This is a typical Indian sadhu (sannyasin) or wandering holy man. You can tell he is a sadhu by his water pot, mala beads and orange robe. You can see some features of his shrine in the background. He will have very few possessions, live in the space next to his shrine and depend on gifts from passers-by to sustain himself.

The Four Aims in Life

Underlying the particular duties of each caste and stage in life Hindus have four basic aims in life which are also expressed in the Law Books of Manu.

- **dharma** - Practising right conduct in religious and social duties

- **arta** - Earning material wealth by honest means and providing for family and society

- **kama** - enjoying the pleasures and beauty of life

- **moksha** - aiming for the final goal of release from the round of rebirth and attaining liberation.

A Hindu who carries out all his or her religious and moral duties according to their stage in life, caste, occupation and financial means is said to be true to his or her dharma.

Gaining wealth by honest means is a valid goal in life for Hindus. This business man looks particularly pleased with himself!

Activities

Key Elements

1 State the main duties of each of the following stages:
Brahmacharya
Grihasta
Vanaprastha
Sannyasin.

2 What is the purpose of each stage of life for the individual and for society?

3 What are the Four Aims in Life for Hindus? Which do you think are the hardest to achieve?

Think About It

4 In what way is the student stage for a Hindu different from the student stage for most young people in the West? How do you see your own life as a student?

5 Do you agree that marriage should be a sacred duty?

6 What are your views on the Hindu attitude to old age? What do you see as its advantages or disadvantages?

Assignments

1 'Hindus have to obey so many rules and perform so many duties that they do not have any individual freedom.'

Do you agree or disagree with the statement? Give reasons for your answer, illustrating it with examples of the duties of Hindus in different castes and at different stages of life, and comparing these duties with those of people who are not Hindu. In giving your views, show that you have considered more than one point of view.

2 From what you have studied in this chapter, illustrate the effect that the Hindu sense of duty has upon social and family life.

2

The Nature of God

- One God: Many Forms
- The Meaning of Brahman
- Brahma, Vishnu and Shiva

- The Goddess
- Popular Deities

One God: Many Forms

A Hindu child asked:
"Grandmother, how many gods are there?"
"There are as many gods as there are creatures, so there must be 300,000,000 gods."
"Grandmother, how many gods are there, really?"
"3000 my child."
"Grandmother, how many gods are there, really?"
"300 my child."
"Grandmother, how many gods are there, really?"
"30 my child."
"Grandmother, how many gods are there, really?"
"3 my child."
"Grandmother, how many gods are there, really?"
"One my child, really."

This conversation reveals the unique way in which Hindus understand the nature of god. For Hindus there is no difficulty in accepting that god is one and yet has many different forms.

Hindus believe that:

- There is one universal spirit called Brahman which pervades the whole universe and is symbolised in the syllable OM.
- There are three main aspects to Brahman, called the Hindu triad of Brahma the creator, Vishnu the preserver and Shiva the destroyer.
- There are human and animal forms of Vishnu, especially Krishna and Rama.
- There are lesser gods or devas which are special to particular places.
- God is seen as present in all life - especially in things that are of service to humanity, like the cow, rivers and trees.
- God dwells in all creatures as the innermost spirit or true self.

The reason why the Hindu idea of the nature of god is expressed in so many varied ways is due to the long history of Hinduism.

The earliest evidence we have for the Hindu idea of God comes from the Indus Valley in 2000 BCE. Archaeologists have found inscriptions which suggest that the inhabitants worshipped fertility gods both male and female.

This clay tablet probably shows an early form of the god Shiva. Although it may be almost 4,000 years old, this same sitting position is still used in meditation. Notice how the god is linked with the idea of fertility - something which continues in the worship of Shiva today (see page 26).

Some scholars say that a famous clay tablet showing a horned deity sitting in a meditation posture with corn growing out of his chest is an early form of the god Shiva. The Aryan people introduced their idea of God to the other inhabitants through their hymns and songs. In these, God is seen as the power within the natural forces of thunder and lightening, the sun, sky, dawn, earth and moon. Later, the priests and hymn-writers formed the idea that the various gods were really different aspects of one supreme power expressed in this famous verse from the Rig Veda.

God is One , but wise men call it by different names.

(*Rig Veda 1.164.46*)

The idea that God is One, but is worshipped in many different forms, is the key to understanding the Hindu idea of God.

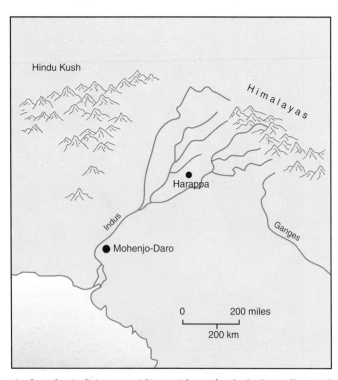

Archaeological sites providing evidence for the Indus valley civilisation.

The Meaning of Brahman

This is an important concept in Hinduism. The word Brahman has its origin in the early scriptures of Hinduism. It comes from the root 'brh' which means 'giving forth' or 'growth and creation'.

When the priests of the early Indian culture tried to harness the powers of nature for their rituals they called the magic power of nature **'brahman'**. Later on it came to mean the life-giving power within the universe. In the scriptures known as the Upanishads Brahman is sometimes described in personal terms as 'He', other times in impersonal terms as 'it'. They say that this power dwells within all living beings in the universe but is also beyond the universe. It is a mysterious truth to grasp and the writers of these scriptures tried to express it in poetry and imagery.

This whole universe is Brahman. Let a man revere it in all tranquillity as that from which all things are born and into which they dissolve and in which they breathe and move.
(Chandogya Upanishad Ch.3 Verse xiv.)

Invisible, intangible, having neither family or caste.
Devoid of eye and ear, devoid of hands and feet.
Eternal, all pervading, penetrating everywhere, most subtle and changeless
The womb and origin of all that comes into being.
(Mundaka Upanishad. Chapter 1, section 1, verse 6.)

For divine and formless is The Person (Brahman)
What is within life and what is outside life are his.
Unborn is He, pure, brilliant,
He is not breath nor mind,
He is the all highest beyond the Imperishable itself.
From Him springs forth the breath of life.
Mind and all the senses too
Sky, wind, light and water
And the earth and all that it sustains.
(Chandogya Upanishad Chapter 2, section I verse 2-3.)

Brilliant it is,
More subtle than all subtle things,
It contains all worlds and indwells all worlds
This is the imperishable Brahman.
This life, this world and mind,
This truth and this immortality
This is a truth that must be pierced my friend.
(Chandogya Upanishad Chapter 2 section ii)

Questions

- Which of these verses describe Brahman in personal terms and impersonal terms?

- What do these verses tell you about the nature of god in Hindu thought?

- Is the idea of Brahman like other ideas of God you have come across?

Brahman is believed to be everywhere and in everything - the origin of all that comes into being, including the light of a new day.

The Sacred Symbol OM

This symbol, consisting of three letters A, U and M, represents the essence of Hinduism and is always seen in temples and shrines. It is considered to be the sacred sound or vibration which is made by the life-giving power of the universe or Brahman. The three syllables are a mantra, a kind of prayer which when uttered with reverence and faith puts the person in touch with their inner nature. It represents many aspects of creation: past, present and future; eternity; birth, life and death; Brahma, Vishnu and Shiva.

Meditation on this sacred syllable satisfies every need and finally leads to liberation.
(Katha Upanishad Chapter 2 , verses 16-17)

OM. The imperishable sound is the seed of all that exists. The past, the present, the future, are all but the unfolding of OM.
(Mandukya Upanishad)

Activities

Key Elements

1 What is the meaning of the following terms?

(i)   OM
(ii)   Upanishads
(iii)   Brahman

Think About It

2 What do you think is meant by 'sacred'? What aspects of your own life do you consider to be sacred?

3 What kind of symbols do you see around you in your daily life? Why are symbols sometimes more helpful than words in communicating a message?

4 Meditation is becoming quite popular today. Why do some people want to practise meditation? What effect do you think it has on them?

Assignments

1 Find some symbols of other religions, look at them carefully and draw them. What are these symbols trying to say about the religion? Does the symbol refer to a teaching or belief which is central to the religion? If so, what is it?

2 The swastika is another symbol found in Hindu temples. This confuses many people from the West, because the swastika is associated with the Nazi party in Germany in the Second World War. Find out what the meaning of this symbol is in Hinduism and how it differs from the meaning given to it by the Nazis. Explain in your own words why the symbol is sacred to Hindus.

The Hindu Triad of Brahma, Vishnu and Shiva

This statue, called a trimurti because it shows three gods in one, represents Brahma, Vishnu and Shiva.

The Hindu triad of gods, Brahma, Vishnu and Shiva are the three aspects of the life force of Brahman: creating, preserving and destroying and re-creating the universe.

Within Hinduism, the continual evolution of the universe follows the same cycle we find in the natural world. Tiny seeds, planted in the ground, form the origins of life and grow into a forest of trees in which the processes of birth, decay, death and rebirth are continually in motion.

At first glance the images of the gods appear bewildering and part of a fantasy world but, as one investigates the meaning of the symbols and images, it is possible not only to appreciate the purpose and meaning of the gods for Hindus, but some of the profound religious truths contained within Hinduism.

The images and pictures of the gods are often richly decorated and embellished. They may have several arms to indicate their many powers and in each hand they hold objects to illustrate their particular powers. Colour is also used to symbolise their nature.

The gods may be accompanied by animals or birds which are their special vehicles to protect them and enable them to move around the cosmos.

The rich and varied symbolism provides keys to help the worshippers to relate to their gods and gain spiritual insight.

Brahma

Brahma, the creator god, is shown with four heads facing the four directions symbolising that he has created the entire universe. After each kalpa or era he meditates in order to recreate the universe and he is guided by the Vedas which he holds in his hand. The water pot or vessel (kamandalu) is used in the ritual of prayer prior to meditation, and is used by men of renunciation who have chosen to withdraw from involvement in the world and direct their attention towards deeper spiritual matters.

The rosary or mala which he holds is also used as an aid to meditation. He may sit on a lotus which is a symbol of purity, as it emerges white and pure in the sunlight untouched by the mud and slime out of which it has grown. He may sit in the meditation posture like a yogi who is unaffected by the world around him.

Shiva

Shiva is the aspect of Brahman which destroys and re-creates the universe and he is shown in several different forms:

- The Lord of the Dance or Nataraja
- The great **yogi** or Maha-Yogi
- The **lingum**.

As Nataraja, Lord of the Dance, Shiva is demonstrating his creative energy in bringing the world into existence and also his power to destroy it.

This image of Shiva Nataraja was specially made for the Cultural Festival of India in 1985.

He dances on the demon dwarf Apasamara Purusha, which represents human pride and ignorance or ego. This needs to be crushed if progress on the spiritual path is to be made.

In one hand he holds an hour-glass shaped rattle drum, the damaru, which represents the pulse of time and the rhythm of the universe which he controls. In another hand he sometimes holds a deer which denotes an unsteady mind which darts hither and thither rather than settling on God. In another hand the holds some flames which symbolises his powers of destruction. In his other hands he is making symbolic gestures or mudras which convey a message. The upraised hand is saying "Do not fear I will protect as I destroy." The hand pointing to the demon shows the destruction of ignorance.

His trailing locks of hair show the frenzy of this dance as his energy swirls about the world. He is surrounded by a circle of fire which expresses the eternal motion of the universe in the process of creation, destruction and re-creation.

Shiva as Maha-Yogi is represented in a human form seated in a meditation posture set against a white background of the snowy Himalayas. These represent the purity of his mind, not distracted by the world as he sits in deep meditation. His posture represents the perfect harmony and serenity of a person's mind when it has gained final peace and liberation through deep meditation.

His half closed eyes show that his mind is focused on his inner self and centred on God consciousness even though his body is in the world. He has a pile of tangled hair in a top knot, rising in a cone on his head, out of which pours the river Ganges next to the crescent moon. This relates to a story in which the river Ganges in its descent to the earth would have destroyed and shattered Shiva had he not caught it in his locks of hair. The crescent moon indicates the coolness and calmness of a yogi in meditation.

His third eye situated in the middle of his forehead signifies his powers of concentration and the wisdom and special insight developed

The shrine to Shiva at the Laxmi Narayan (Birla) Temple in Delhi; the animals depicted towards the front of the shrine indicate that he is Lord of all the Animals.

Shiva as represented in the Lingum. This is a symbol of Shiva's energy and power to generate and regenerate life. In some of the myths Shiva's lingum or phallus is described as a cosmic pillar reaching into space at one end and into the bowels of the earth at the other end. Thus it represents cosmic power and light. It is in this form that Shiva is shown in shrines and temples and in which he is able to receive worship. In these temples Shiva's vehicle, Nandi the bull, is the protector of the god and the doorkeeper of the temple.

by all yogis and especially the great yogi, Shiva. His complexion is blue, relating to another story in which he drank poison in order to save the world from being destroyed by evil. Blue also symbolises the infinity of the sky and the oceans.

He is often draped in a tiger skin, which symbolises the need to overcome arrogant pride and Shiva's power to destroy evil and ignorance. Similarly, the serpent coiled around his neck or body shows his powers to control his desires and ego. He holds the trident which is a sign of a holy man, a symbol of asceticism or withdrawing from the pleasures of worldly life.

This is a Shiva lingum outside the 18th century temple at Ghrishneshwar, north of Aurangabad.

These pilgrims are visiting the temple and are paying respect to Nandi the bull, Shiva's vehicle, who guards the entrance to the temple.

Vishnu

'Vishnu' comes from a word meaning pervading. His function in the Hindu triad of gods is to maintain and preserve the order and harmony of the universe. He is shown lying on a many headed cobra (Ananta) which symbolises cosmic energy and cosmic time. Vishnu arises out of an ocean of milk (Ananda) which conveys endless bliss and endless mind. His colour is blue to indicate he is as infinite and endless as the sky.

In one of his four hands he holds the discus or chakra to show he maintains the order and righteousness in the universe. In another he holds the conch shell (shanha) which, because of the deep humming sound it makes when held next to the ear, denotes the music of the cosmos, calling people to lead a pure and spiritual life. He also holds the mace and wears a crown to indicate his kingly authority and ability to protect the world and remove its evil.

He is sometimes shown sitting on a lotus which is a symbol of the beauty and purity of the universe. His vehicle is Garuda, a man-eagle, which is a symbol of strength, power and piety. All the symbols of Vishnu are intended to remind the worshipper of the need to follow religious and moral laws and to take notice of spiritual values to prevent suffering and disaster taking over the world.

Activities

Think About It

1 The Hindu triad of Brahma, Shiva and Vishnu is sometimes called the Hindu Trinity. Why do you think this is so?

2 What are the functions of these three gods in the cycle of life and why are they shown with so many arms?

3 In Hinduism, it is accepted that the universe is created, destroyed and re-created. How does this differ from the view of creation and the end of the world that is accepted by some people in the West?

4 Why do you think there are different beliefs in the East and the West about the origin and the end of the world?

5 How do you think 'the end of the world' might come about?

6 Both Brahma and Shiva withdraw from the world and develop their wisdom and spiritual powers through meditation. Why might it be necessary to withdraw from the world in order to develop the spiritual side of one's nature? What kind of distractions exist in the everyday world?

The Goddess

Hinduism is unique in the great importance it gives to the goddess, which is widely worshipped in India in a variety of forms.

The Vedic scriptures refer to the goddess as the creative energy of **shakti**, as the activating force which enables the male gods to exert their power. Shakti is like the yeast which is added when baking bread; although the ingredients are present, the bread could not be formed without the vital energy of the yeast. So, without the creative energy of Shakti, the universe would not be full of life.

The goddess has many forms and is sometimes depicted on her own as Durga or Kali, or as the consort or wife of the male gods Vishnu, Shiva and Brahma.

Durga and Kali

These two forms of the goddess reveal her powers to destroy evil and ignorance.

As Durga she appears as a brave heroine riding a tiger to show she can control this wild and arrogant animal and harness its strength. She carries many ferocious weapons in her many arms in order to kill the demon buffalo which represents ignorance and selfishness.

As Kali the goddess is shown in her most terrifying form. She embodies the power of destruction and punishes all evil doers by annihilating them.

She is often depicted as dark or black in colour, with a red face and her tongue hanging out, a garland of skulls around her neck and a severed head in her hand. This is to frighten evil enemies.

This is strange imagery for a goddess, and is intended to show her mercilessness in killing all forms of evil and ignorance. Both Kali and Durga, in the midst of their frightening aspects, have one hand raised in the mudra meaning "Do not fear, I will protect you and goodness will replace evil."

Question

- There are very few religions to-day in which the goddess is worshipped. Why do you think this is so?

Goddesses as consorts of the gods

Parvati or Uma

A statuette of Shiva and Parvati

Lakshmi

She is the consort of Shiva and reveals the kind and gentle aspect of the goddess with all the finest qualities of a loyal and loving wife.

She is most often shown in the company of Shiva and holds a lotus in her hand and the mudra offering protection or gifts.

Lakshmi

She is the consort of Vishnu and represents the beauty, prosperity and benevolence of the goddess.

She is shown standing or sitting on a lotus with gold coins pouring out of one of her hands and lotus flowers in the others. She wears lots of gold jewellery and a pink sari or pink lotus flowers, as pink is the colour of kindness.

She is the goddess of good fortune and Hindus pray to her when they need help with money and especially at Divali when they hope for a prosperous New Year.

Saraswati

Saraṣwati is the consort of Brahma and the goddess of knowledge. This is not just intellectual knowledge but the knowledge revealed in the scriptures about the inner self and the nature of Brahman.

She sits on a lotus and holds sacred scriptures in one hand, mala prayer beads in another, a lotus in another and also plays the vina or Indian lute. This music represents the music of the spheres or the cosmos expressed in the syllable OM.

So this aspect of the goddess reminds Hindus of the importance of prayer, study of the scriptures and purity of mind. Her vehicle is the swan, an appropriately graceful and beautiful pure white bird.

Question

- Why is the goddess so important in Hinduism? What are the special powers of these goddesses?

Popular deities

In Hinduism the idea of God is very complex, so in order to help people relate to it, the many aspects of God are represented in human and animal form.

The most important of these are the nine **avatars** of Vishnu. Avatar is sometimes translated as incarnation, but it means more than that. It refers to the power of God to take any form at all, or the descent of God to the earthly realm in any form to perform a special task.

In the Bhagavad Gita it says that the divine powers enter human affairs when there is decay of righteousness, goodness and harmony in the world, and when evil forces and influences take over human affairs.

I will come forth for the protection of the good
For the destruction of evil doers
For the sake of firmly establishing righteousness
For this purpose I am born from age to age.
(Bhagavad Gita Chapter IV verses 7-8)

The ten principal avatars are:

1 **The Fish, Matsya**

2 **The Tortoise, Kurma**

3 **The Boar, Varaha**

4 **The man-lion, Narashinha**

5 **The dwarf, Vamana**

6 **Rama, (Parasu-rama) the warrior with the battle axe**

7 **Rama, the prince**

8 **Krishna**

9 **Buddha**

10 **Kalki.**

There are many accounts of the avatars in the Bhagavad Purana, a collection of stories and legends about the popular gods. These stories about the avatars all contain the same theme, that of rescuing all living beings, both human and animal, from evil and harmful forces, whether natural or demonic.

Questions

1 What are the signs of the decay of righteousness in our world today?

2 In what ways can righteousness be restored?

3 Does religion help to restore righteousness in the world?

Extension Work

Read the accounts of the heroic events of these avatars and answer the questions at the end of the section.

Matsya the fish rescued Manu, the ancestor the human race, from a flood.

Kurma the tortiose provided his curved back as a support for a mountain from which the gods and demons churned up the waters of the ocean in order to extract the most important ingredients for life, which had been lost in a flood. These included amrit (the nectar of immortality), Lakshmi the goddess of wealth and beauty, the divine cow, a precious gem, an elephant and a conch shell which would bring victory in battle to anyone who found it.

Varaha the boar, using his tusks, rescued the earth after it had been pushed to the bottom of the ocean by a demon.

Narashimha the man lion came into being when a demon called Hiranyankasipu ruled the earth. This demon had magical powers so that he could not be killed by any means. The demon did not believe in God, but his son Prahlada did, so the demon tortured him. Narashimha waited until sunset and emerged from a stone pillar at the entrance of the demon's house and killed the demon by tearing him to pieces, so Prahlada was free to worship God in peace.

Vamana the dwarf appeared when another demon controlled the earth. He approached the demon and asked if he could have all the land he could cover in three steps. Seeing the small size of the dwarf, he agreed. Then Vamana grew to an enormous size and with two paces he covered the earth and the heavens. With the third step he pressed the demon into the underworld.

Parasurama (Rama with the axe) saved the priests of the faith when they were threatened with destruction by the warriors or kshatriyas. He exterminated twenty-one generations of the Kshatriya race because of their arrogance and also taught the lesson that a father's command must be obeyed.

Rama the prince came into being when the demon king Ravanna of Sri Lanka ruled the earth. Rama had been tricked out of becoming king and was exiled to the forest for fourteen years with his wife Sita and his brother Lakshmana. While they were living in the forest Sita was kidnapped by Ravanna. With help from the monkey God Hanuman, Rama was able to destroy the evil king Ravanna, rescue Sita and restore peace and happiness to the earth.

Krishna is one of the most popular avatars and the stories about him reveal his powers to overcome all kinds of evil and establish goodness and harmony on the earth. His teachings are contained in the Bhagavad Gita.

Buddha appeared as a great teacher and taught the doctrine of ahimsa (harmlessness) so that no creature should be killed. His purpose was to protect the animals.

Kalki is the avatar of Vishnu which is yet to come when evil takes over the world again. It is said that he will come on a white horse carrying a shining sword to destroy evil.

Although these stories might seem quite fantastic, some Indian scholars have related them to the various stages of evolution, the fish relating to the amphibian stage, then the animal stage with the boar, then the half-man, half-animal with the dwarf, then the aggressive warlike man with Parasurama, then a perfect man with Rama the prince, then a full manifestation of divinity with Krishna. This suggests that there is a deeper meaning to these stories than one might assume at first glance.

1 What are the common themes in all these stories?

2 Can you see parallels between the different avatars and the stages of evolution? Explain them in your own words.

Krishna

Krishna is the most popular avatar of Vishnu and is worshipped as a god in his own right. According to one Hindu writer

> *Krishna is a living force even today. Sages, saints and scholars have glorified him as the complete manifestation of divinity. He has entered into our song, dance and poetry and every aspect of our culture.*

The legends about his life are contained in the Bhagavad Purana and his teachings are found in the Bhagavad Gita, which is part of the Mahabharata.

> *His life is seen as the Bhagavad Gita in action. He is the ideal child, student, lover, husband, warrior, teacher and king.*

The word Krishna in Sanskrit means dark, referring to the inner self or atman within a person who is unaware of god's true nature. He is blue in colour, representing the infinity of his divine nature, and clothed in yellow to suggest the earth and so show he is really god in earthly form.

In the stories about his life it is said that he was born in a jail in the state of Mathura which was ruled by his cruel tyrant of an uncle, Kamsa, who had taken the throne from his parents. As a baby Krishna was miraculously rescued and taken to live in Vrindabran in Gokula (Cow village) where he was brought up by simple peasant foster parents, Yashoda and Nandi.

Krishna's divine nature was revealed through various accounts of his childhood pranks. One day Yashoda scolded him for swallowing some mud, but when she looked into his open mouth to find the earth, she saw the whole universe and had to worship him as a god.

Another story tells of how he overcame a many headed serpent or dragon, Kaliya, who had been causing the entire village to suffer by polluting the river with poison. In the ensuing battle Krishna leapt onto the serpent's hood, danced on it and tormented the serpent so much with his divine weight so that the serpent had to ask forgiveness and become a worshipper of Krishna. The image of Krishna dancing on a serpent's head shows his powers to overcome evil.

Radha and Krishna

Krishna is often shown playing the flute. This represents the enchanting music which evokes the bliss of realising the true nature of God. The milkmaids or gopis of Vrindabran were enchanted by Krishna's divine music and danced in ecstasy around him. Peacocks also opened their feathers which is a symbol of their joy and ecstasy. The gopis remembered him throughout the day when engaged in all their activities. When he disappeared from view, they would constantly repeat his name, imitate his gestures and dancing, and sing his praises in many hymns until he reappeared to dance with them. This represents the way in which Krishna's worshippers express their love for him. His favourite gopi was Radha and the complete devotion of Krishna for Radha and Radha for Krishna represents the unending love of God for his devotees and the devotees' complete submission to God. Thus Krishna and Radha are often found as the divine couple in Hindu temples and shrines.

This kind of devotion and worship is called **bhakti** and is particularly associated with worship of Krishna. Vrindabran is a place of pilgrimage for Krishna devotees as it is considered to be the actual place where all his exploits took place.

The stories of Krishna's life relate how he left the village of Vrindabran to reclaim his kingly rights from the evil tryant Kamsa. Through his efforts he destroyed the evil powers and established peace and order in the land of Mathura. Thus Krishna is shown wearing a crown to depict his qualities as righteous monarch guarding the welfare of all beings.

Of all the Hindu gods, Krishna is the best known in the West.

The International Society for Krishna Consciousness (ISCON) started in the 1960s, but its origins go back to the 16th century. This movement opened up Hinduism to westerners. Its members are devoted to Lord Krishna and submit themselves in love and devotion to him. They are often seen in western cities chanting Hare Krishna. They encourage vegetarianism, with their special cafes offering free food to those in need.

A western Hindu sitting outside the International ISCON temple at Vrindabran.

Questions

1 Why is Krishna such a popular Indian deity?

2 What is the meaning of these symbols which are often associated with Krishna: blue skin, yellow garments, peacock feather, a bejewelled crown, a flute, a white calf?

3 What is meant by bhakti?

4 How might devotees of Krishna show their devotion for Him?

Extension Work

5 The Krishna Consciousness movement is well established in Britain. They are happy to explain their beliefs and devotion to Lord Krishna. Find out as much as you can about them.

Rama

Rama is another very popular avatar of Vishnu. He is considered to be one of the most glorious of all the characters in the *Ramayana*, the epic in which most of the stories about Rama are found.

In his earthly form he was born as the eldest son of King Dasaratha and he was renowned for his proficiency in archery. His bow and arrow are his weapons to fight against evil. He carries them at all times to show his readiness and alertness to fight against injustice and to establish peace and justice. In the stories about the life of Rama, he is the ideal human being providing a role model as a perfect son, an ideal king, a true husband, a real friend and a noble enemy. His wife Sita represents the qualities of loyalty, caring and devotion that the ideal wife should have.

The Ramayana gives an account of a famous story about Rama which is celebrated at the festival of Divali.

On the eve of Rama's coronation in the the city of Ayodhya, his step mother Kaikeyi demanded that her son Bharat be crowned and that Rama be sent to the forest for fourteen years. Rama knew that his father, the ageing king Dasaratha, would not survive the sorrow and so he left. Here Rama is depicted as an ideal son, as it is a son's duty to fulfil his father's promise in spite of obstacles and Rama would not compromise with the fulfilment of duty.

During the exile of Rama, Sita and his brother Laksmana in the forest, the demon king of Sri Lanka, Ravanna, kidnapped Sita and took her away to his kingdom. Rama made enormous efforts to find her and, with the help of Hanuman king of the monkeys and all the animals of the forest, he attempted to rescue her.

After many heroic events including building an enormous bridge to Lanka, the evil king Ravanna was overcome and Sita was rescued.

Rama with Sita, Lakshmana and Hanuman, the principal characters in the Ramayana epic.

Sita was concerned to show that she had been completely faithful to her husband and was willing to walk through flames to prove her faithfulness. However, Rama rescued her and they both returned to establish a peaceful and prosperous kingdom in Ayodhya.

Sita is considered to be an avatar of the goddess Lakshmi and so her qualities of courage, faithfulness and ability to bring abundance of wealth to the kingdom correspond to the special powers of the deity Lakshmi.

The evil king Ravanna is often shown with ten heads. This can be seen as a symbol of all the knowledge which he had acquired, but which he used for harm rather than good. He had become proud and arrogant. In this way he represents the pride and self importance in human nature. In defeating Ravanna, Rama's victory can be seen as the triumph of goodness and kindness in human nature over anger and pride. The story can be understood in a variety of ways, as a wonderful mythical tale in which goodness triumphs over evil, or as the battle within the human personality to become a better person and acknowledge the reality of God within oneself and in the universe.

Ganesha

At first the image of this god is very puzzling, but when one finds out the meaning of the symbols and the stories which explain them it is possible to appreciate why this god is so important to Hindus.

The name Ganesha in Sanskrit means 'multitude', and Isa means 'Lord', so his name means 'Lord of all Beings'. Since Ganesha is the first son of Lord Shiva this is an appropriate title for him. He is known by other names as well, such as Ganapati, and Gajanana. Gaja means 'elephant', anana means 'face', so Gajanana means 'elephant-faced'. Ganesha is the god of obstacles and people pray to him to remove obstacles from their lives. His statue is found at city gates, or guarding temple doorways and house doors, as he represents the doorkeeper of the universe.

There is a story of how Ganesha received his elephant head. He was moulded from clay by Parvati to guard her bathroom door. Her husband Shiva came to her one night but the door was guarded by Ganesha, who did not allow him to go into Parvati's room. Shiva was so angry at being refused access that he cut off Ganesha's head. Howver Parvati was so distressed that in remorse Shiva replaced it with the head of an elephant. In another version of the story, Parvati made an image of a child with an elephant's head and threw it into the river Ganges where it was brought to life.

In one story Ganesha was said to have lost his trunk in a fight. Therefore many statues show him holding it in his hand like a pen. The pen represents scholarship and wisdom, so Ganesha is considered to be the author of the sacred Vedic scriptures.

Ganesha is usually pictured as having a human form with an elephant head. One tusk is broken, he has a conspicuously large stomach, he sits with one leg folded in and at his feet a variety of food is laid out. A rat sits near the food and looks up at him as if asking permission to eat the food. All these symbols represent the ways to reach the state of human perfection and realisation of God.

Ganesha

- **His large ears and head** indicate his great wisdom which has been acquired by listening carefully to the eternal truths of the Vedic scriptures.
- **The elephant's trunk** is like a very special tool as the elephant can pick up trees with it as well as pick up tiny objects from the ground. So it is a symbol of the intellect which can discriminate and distinguish between truth and falsehood.
- **The large stomach** suggests that Ganesha can 'digest' whatever experiences he undergoes, so that he is not overcome with the losses, suffering and grief of life or carried away with his successes and achievements.
- **One leg folded and the other on the ground** show the two aspects of his personality in balance. One side is firmly rooted in worldly things and the other is engaged in meditation and concentration on God and the inner spiritual self.
- **The food at his feet** denotes the wealth, power and prosperity which he has at his command but which do not rule his life.

• **The rat** represents greed and desire as the rat hoards more than it needs and steals from others. The rat looks for guidance from Ganesha to overcome his greedy desires in order to find the spiritual path to perfection. The rat is Ganesha's vehicle, showing that the overcoming of desires provides enough strength to transport even an elephant.

In each of his four arms Ganesha holds an object which symbolises the path to God-realisation. The **axe** represents the destruction of selfish desires, **the rope** is a means to pull the person away from worldly attachments, the **rice bowl** shows the rewards of spiritual seeking, and the **lotus** is a symbol of the purity of the mind in a person who has reached the final goal.

Throughout India, in all sorts of places – shop windows, advertising hoardings, road junctions – one will find images of deities. Here is an example of the traditional image of Ganesha used in popular folk art.

Activities

Key Elements

1 What are the functions of Brahma, Vishnu, and Shiva in the Hindu Triad of Gods?

2 Choose one these gods and explain the meaning of the symbols associated with him.

3 Krishna and Rama are avatars of the god Vishnu. What is meant by the term avatar?

4 What effect might a belief in these gods have on a Hindu's attitude to:

 (i) the way they behave in this life

 (ii) the universe around them

 (iii) their purpose in this life ?

Think About It

5 Do you think that Hindus believe in one god or in many gods? Give reasons for your answer.

6 In order to find their own way to God, Hindus can choose their own favourite deity as a focus for devotion. They will choose a god with qualities that appeal to them or suit their needs. Suggest some reasons why Krishna, Rama and Ganesha might be chosen as a focus for worship.

7 Hindus have no difficulty in believing that God might take human or animal form. What do you think about this possibility?

8 In Hinduism, individuals might show devotion to a personal god as well as developing their spiritual life through meditation in order to reach the final goal of becoming one with the impersonal absolute, Brahman. What is meant by a personal god? Why might some Hindus find it easier to express devotion to a personal god than to meditate on Brahman?

9 'It is extremely difficult to understand the Hindu concept of God unless you are a Hindu yourself.' Do you agree or disagree with this statement? Give reasons for your answer.

Assignments

1 (a) Choose either Krishna or Rama. Give an account of a story associated with them and name three symbols which would enable you to recognise the deity.

(b) Explain their special powers through the stories and symbols associated with them.

(c) How might devotion to this deity affect a Hindu's behaviour in everyday life?

(d) 'Krishna is the most popular deity in Hinduism.' Do you agree or diasagree with this view? Give reasons for your answer, showing you have considered more than one point of view.

2 (a) Choose two of these Hindu goddesses: Kali, Durga, Parvati, Saraswati, Lakshmi. Describe the main features of these goddesses as shown in the symbols associated with them.

(b) Explain why the worship of the goddess is found in Hinduism.

(c) 'It is impossible to think of God in a female form.' Do you agree or disagree with this view? Give reasons for your answer.

3 It has been said that Hinduism is the religion of 300,000,000 gods.

(a) Explain why Hindus appear to worship so many gods.

(b) What does the concept of Brahman and the OM symbol reveal about the Hindu understanding of God?

3

God, Humanity and the Natural World

Every religion deals with fundamental questions and concerns we have about the purpose of human existence and the whole of the material universe:
• What is a human being and its place in the universe?
• What happens to us when we die?
• What kind of destiny awaits all living beings?
• What causes suffering and misfortune to occur in the world?

• Do animals have souls?
• Where did the universe come from?
• Is there an end to the world?
• What is the final and ultimate goal of life?

Hindu religious philosophy offers some very profound insights and answers to these questions. Some Hindu beliefs are very different from those commonly found in the West; others are very similar.

The Nature of the True Self or Atman

Before many of the fundamental questions of life can be approached there has to be a basic understanding of what a human being is made up of. Most religions accept the existence of some kind of spirit or soul dwelling in each person, which is their divine nature or the spark of the presence of God within them.

Hinduism asserts this truth in a very convincing way with one of its most profound teachings about the nature of the true self or Atman. For Hindus a person is not only a soul within a body, but a true, eternal, perfect self within a temporary and imperfect body. This atman is described in many ways in the Upanishads and the Bhagavad Gita. When the body dies the atman, as the eternal, indestructable essence of the living being, leaves the body and enters another body – a process called reincarnation.

> Finite they say are these our bodies indwelt by an eternal embodied self,
> for this self is indestructible incommensurable...
>
> Who thinks this self can be a slayer
> Who thinks that it can be slain
> Both of these have no right knowledge: it does not slay nor is it slain
> As a man casts off his worn out clothes and takes on other new ones
> So does the embodied self cast off its worn out bodies and enters other new ones.
> Weapons do not cut it nor does fire burn it
> The waters do not wet it nor does the wind dry it
> Uncuttable, unburnable, unwettable, undryable it is —
> Eternal, roving everywhere, firm set, unmoved, primeval
>
> Bhagavad Gita, Chapter 2 verses 19-24

Katha Upanishad

This tells an ancient story about Nachiketas the son of a poor brahmin. He is dissatisfied with the gifts his father has offered to the sacrificial priests and insists that he be offered instead. His father in a rage cries

> Alright, to Yama the King of Death I give you.

Arriving in the realm of Yama, Nachiketas finds himself absent and has to wait without food for three days and nights. Yama on his return grants the boy three wishes in recompense. Nachiketas's third wish is to know how the truth about the nature of the self and how the cycle of death and rebirth may be overcome. This is what Yama replied:

> (The atman is...)
> More subtle than the subtle, greater than the great
> The self is hidden in the heart of all creatures here...
> This is the self deep hidden in all beings.
> Yet it can be seen by men who see things subtle.
> Katha Upanishad, Chapter 2, verse 20

Knowledge of this true self is hidden from most people as it can only be discovered by contemplation of the scriptures, and the development of spiritual insight through meditation. The Hindu seers say if everyone had this knowledge of the real nature of the human soul, there would be no problems in the world, as everyone would be happy, having experienced wisdom, peacefulness and bliss.

The Upanishads describe the various layers which cover up the atman and mask its true nature. These veils have to be lifted through the process of insight and meditation and contemplation of the inner self. This process leads to the realisation that the true self is the same reality as Brahman, the life force which pervades the whole universe. This realisation is a very profound and transforming experience. The seeker after truth enters into a special state of wisdom and feels a sense of unity with the universe and discovers at the depth of their being the individual atman or self is the same as the atman of the universe. That is why the Upanishads proclaim such truths as

> I am Brahman,
> Thou art That.

He is my self within my heart smaller than a grain of rice or a barley corn, or a mustard seed, or a grain of millet, or the kernel of a grain of millet; this is my Self within my heart greater than the earth, greater than the atmosphere, greater than the sky greater than all these worlds.

This my self within my heart is that Brahman. When I depart from hence I shall merge into it. He who believes this will never doubt.

Chandogya Upanishad Section 11
Chapter xiv verse 4-5

This is Sri Yanta. A Yanta is an abstract design or pattern which expresses an idea. In this example, it expresses the truth that the inner self is the same as the universal soul.

Indian philosophers have debated and speculated about the nature of this inner self atman and how it relates to or is part of the universal spirit Brahman. Are they the same energy or are they separate, distinct and different? One of the greatest Indian religious teachers was Shankara who lived in the ninth century CE. He founded a school of thought called Advaita Vedanta which means 'non-dualism' and which said that at the inner self of all individual living beings was the same energy which gave life to the universe.

Each atman goes though a series of lives until it is liberated from the cycle of death and rebirth when it merges with Brahman. Other philosophers such as Ramanuja and Madhva claimed that the atman did not merge with Brahman but remained quite separate.

Questions

1 What do you think your true self is?

2 Which aspects of human nature stay the same, and which change?

3 Do you think the Hindu belief in the self affects their outlook on life?

Another teaching found in Hindu scriptures gives us some insights into the relationship between the body and the soul. According to the school of thought known as Samkyha yoga, we are made up of matter (prakriti) and spirit (purusha). The spiritual element is eternal, pure and indestructible but it is trapped in matter. Matter is classified in a very complex system of elements including air fire water earth and space.

One interesting aspect of this is the three qualities which help to form character and personality in all living beings. These are called **gunas** and are:

- **sattva** (the qualities of light, knowledge, goodness and seeking for truth)
- **rajas** (the forces of energy, ambition, and desires)
- **tamas** (the forces of darkness, ignorance and heaviness.)

It is these aspects of our physical nature which incline us to certain kinds of action and behaviour and eventually determine the future destiny of the atman.

The following stories from the Upanishads reveal the teaching that atman (the true self) and Brahman (the spirit within the universe) are the same reality.

"Bring me a fig."
"Here is one."
"Break it."
" I have."
" What do you see there?"
" Seeds, very tiny."
"Break one of them."
"I have."
"What do you see there?"
"Nothing."

"My son , the subtle essence is there, and you do not see it. It is by this essence that the tree stands up, tall though it is.

"Be it confident my dear son. The whole universe is identified with that subtle essence which is none other than the self. And you are that Svetaketu."

"Father teach me more," he asked.
"Be it so", his father replied.

"Place this salt in water, and then come to me in the morning."
Svetaketu did as he was asked, and next morning his father said to him
"Bring me the salt which you placed in the water last night."
The son looked for it, but could not find it because it had dissolved completely.
"Sip the water from the surface", said the father
"How is it?"
"It is salt."
"Sip it from the middle," said the father. "How is it?"
" It is salt."
"Sip it from the bottom," said the father. "How is it?"
"It is salt".
His father explained.
"In the same manner, my dear son, you do not see Being, but it is there. It is this subtle essence. The whole universe is identified with it, and it is none other than the self. And you are that Svetaketu."
Chandogya Upanishad 6:3-18

The Sacredness of the Natural World

The Hindu understanding of the nature of God as the life-giving energy which pervades the universe and dwells within every living being, naturally gives rise to a sense of the sacredness of all forms of life. All the natural elements which are essentially life-giving, such as rivers, trees or plants are sometimes worshipped as living deities.

The belief and practice of **ahimsa** is a basic principle in Hinduism. It means more than non-violence, but an attitude of love and reverence for all other beings. It springs from a deep respect for the essence of life which is central to Hinduism. Hindus believe that God is in everything and that animals as well humans have souls. It is for this reason that Hindus are vegetarian.

Trees being worshipped during Karttik (Karttik is the name of the month that runs from mid-October to mid-November). In this village ceremony, women are tying galtas around a sacred tree. Many trees are considered sacred in India, especially banyan and pipal trees.

Many Hindus regard Vishnu as the supreme God, the creator and preserver or maintainer of the universe. Vishnu is often depicted asleep on the coils of the many headed cobra Ananta, a name which means 'without end'. The serpent itself is resting on a great ocean, representing the time before the world came into being. At the end of this time of sleeping, Vishnu decides to reproduce the world again, so he gently stirs the water of the great ocean. From this beginning, the five elements of creation develop, then the sounds, and then all the worlds come into existence.

Puja at Buddhanilakanth, a Hindu temple in Katmandu, Nepal. This photograph shows part of a huge statue of the sleeping Vishnu. He lies upon a sleeping serpent, Ananta. These devotees are making offerings of milk by pouring it into Vishnu's mouth. Notice the mace. Why is this a symbol of Vishnu?

The sacred cow

Most notable in Hinduism is the reverence for the cow which nurtures and sustains life in the village. Its milk provides essential food and nourishment, its dung provides fuel, heat and light, even its urine has medicinal qualities.

Gandhi said that the cow was a symbol of Hinduism. Most Hindus are vegetarian as killing animals is against the principle of ahimsa, and Hindus believe in total harmlessness to all living creatures .

> *A teacher of the scriptures, father, mother, guru, brahmin, cow and ascetic — they should never be killed.*
>
> *Law of Manu*

Questions

1 What reasons would a Hindu give for not killing a cow or eating beef?

2 Why are trees and rivers considered to be sacred and like deities to Hindus?

3 Which of the following characteristics dominates your character:

(i)   sattva - goodness, kindness

(ii) rajas - energy and passion

(iii) tamas - darkness and sleepiness?

Concern for the created world

Respect for and proptection of the environment is considered to be a religious duty in Hindu scriptures.

This village is in a fertile part of India, and these women are carrying baskets of cow dung to their village. Cow dung is essential to village life as it fertilises the soil and is dried out to create cow pats which are used for fuel. It is easy to see why the cow is regarded as sacred in such a rural setting.

The Sri Ganga temple at Hardwar. This illustrates how religious devotion is part of everyday life and the way in which Hindus like to gather together in such holy places. These temples are sited along the river, which is itself considered to be a goddess. Notice the shape of the shikhara tower and the flags which mark the place of the inner shrine.

Sunrise is a traditional time for prayer in many religions. It is the fresh start to a new day and a celebration of the renewal of life. It is the religious duty of brahmins to preserve these traditions.

In the photograph on the right, the brahmin's hands are raised in a special mudra, paying homage to the sun. He is wearing special robes and is marked with three horizontal lines to show his devotion to the god Shiva.

Questions

1 How can religious devotion be part of everyday life?

2 Why do so many religions encourage the practice of morning prayers?

3 Does it really matter what time and place people choose for worship?

A brahmin performs dawn rituals at Varanasi.

In this photograph, three images of lifegiving powers come together: the cow, the Shiva lingum (the symbol of reproduction) and the yoni (which represents Shakti, the female power and creative energy).

Activities

Key Elements

1 What is meant by 'atman'?

2 What is the relationship between atman and Brahman in the Upanishads?

3 What does Samkhya yoga teach about matter and spirit?

Think About It

4 The western world is too concerned about material well-being and physical comforts, and forgets the spiritual side of human nature. In contrast, Hinduism puts spiritual life first. What do you think?

Assignment

(a) Explain the Hindu belief in 'the true self.'

(b) How does this belief affect Hindus' attitude towards (i) their destiny and (ii) the natural world?

(c) 'Hindus have neglected material progess for the sake of spiritual experience.' Do you think this is a fair statement to make about Hinduism?

4

Human Life and Liberation

- Samsara
- Karma and Human Destiny

- Moksha: Human Freedom
- Yoga

The teachings of Hinduism address some of the fundamental concerns of all human beings:

- What is the purpose of my life?
- What is the reason for human existence?
- Why are some people in the world rich, happy and successful and others suffer?
- What is my destiny and can I control it?
- What happens to me when I die?
- How has the past influenced the present and how will it influence the future?

The answers are found in the Hindu beliefs of samsara, karma and moksha. The basis of these beliefs lies in the Hindu understanding of the relationship between the body and the soul, or atman. The body belongs to the material world which is always changing and is imperfect, and possibly a kind of dream or illusion, whereas the atman is part of the spiritual reality of Brahman and the ultimate truth.

Samsara

Samsara means 'wandering' and so refers to the wanderings of the soul from body to body, in one lifetime after another. Samsara refers to this cycle of existence of birth, death and rebirth. The laws of nature demonstrate this process when the new buds appear on the trees every spring even though they appeared to die the previous winter.

For sure is the death of all that is born, sure is the birth of all that dies: so in a matter that no one can prevent, you have no cause to grieve.
Bhagavad Gita Chapter 2 verse 27.

Samsara is a kind of recycling process. Hindus believe that the whole of the universe is subject to the re-cycling process of birth, death and rebirth. The universe has come into existence many times, disintegrated and then reformed from the basic elements. So there are many beginnings and endings to life and not just one lifetime. This is applied to all living beings.

For human beings the soul or atman is caught in the human body and is continually reborn in countless lives, possibly as many as 8,400,000, until the atman or soul escapes the trap of samsara. So, whereas to some people in the West the idea of having another chance to enjoy earthly existence seems attractive, to Hindus samsara is seen as a curse. The expression "Stop the world I want to get off" more clearly reflects the Hindu view of samsara.

The purpose of the each life time is to perfect one's wisdom and purity of mind and heart so that the atman is freed from the body and the material world and can reach the final goal, which is called **moksha**. This is like trying to make gold from impure metals; it takes many attempts, but with persistence the perfect gold is extracted.

However, the reason why humans and all other living beings are continually reborn is based in the Hindu belief in karma.

Karma and Human Destiny

Karma means 'action' and the law of karma is the law of cause and effect. Hindus believe that this life may not have been our first one, and we may have been born many times in the past. The karma from previous lives leaves an impression which is carried over into the next life, so evil or selfish actions will result in a life full of suffering, while unselfish action and generous intentions will result in a happy and fortunate life.

Thus, to Hindus, nothing can happen by accident. Everything that happens to a person in this life has been caused by some action or thought in the past. Even if someone might appear to 'get away with murder', Hindus believe that they will pay for it one day.

What a man becomes in this in his next life depends upon his karma. By good deeds he attains merit, by bad actions he becomes evil. The karma of a man ruled by desire attaches to his atman, so that he is forced to suffer rebirth and return to the world of men. When all attachment arising from desires is destroyed, man's mortality ends and only then does atman reach Brahman (i.e. attains liberation, moksha).
Brihad-aranyaka Upanishad. IV. 4. Verses 3,5,2

As a man casts off his worn out clothes
And takes other new ones in their place
So does the embodied soul cast off his worn out bodies
And enters others new.
Bhagavad Gita. Chapter 2 verse 22

It is not uncommon to see beggars and cripples in India, especially at places of pilgrimage, and providing for those in need is regarded as an important duty for Hindus.
It is often quite a shocking and upsetting sight for people in wealthy countries to see the poverty and suffering of people in developing countries. In the West, people's attitude to suffering is to see it as a great misfortune. For those Hindus who believe in the Law of Karma and reincarnation, suffering and misfortune are due to bad deeds in a former existence.

For a Hindu, this belief could provide a strong incentive to live a good, moral life and to fulfil the duties of one's dharma. Although one's destiny in this life might be influenced by past deeds, one can also take responsibility for one's future destiny. The law of karma also explains all the differences in circumstances and inequalities amongst people.

In India, the caste system can be linked to the law of karma, as being born into a lowly caste could be seen as a result of previous deeds.

Even though modern Hindus regard the caste system as outmoded, more traditional Hindus can justify it as a result of the law of karma.

Those whose conduct on earth has given pleasure can hope to enter a pleasant womb, that is the womb of a brahmin, or a woman of the princely class, or a woman of the peasant class; but those whose conduct on earth has been foul can expect to enter a foul and stinking womb, that is the womb of a bitch or a pig or an outcaste.

Chandogya Upanishad V x, verse 7

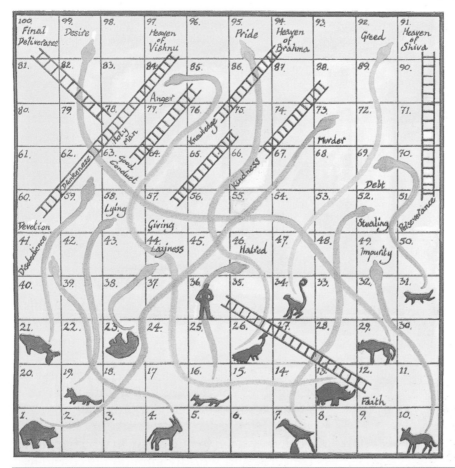

Snakes and ladders is a traditional Hindu game and is a good way of teaching and explaining how the law of karma operates. Here it can be seen that very evil deeds can result in rebirth in an animal form.

Questions

1 What aspects of the natural world show the process of life, death and rebirth?

2 Why do Hindus think samsara is a curse?

3 What effect would belief in karma have on a Hindu's moral attitudes and behaviour?

4 How might belief in karma help Hindus accept their own suffering and the suffering of others?

5 Does the law of karma explain all the differences and inequalities in the world? What other explanations could be given?

Moksha: Human Freedom

Although many Hindus aspire to a good rebirth, the ultimate goal in life is for the atman or soul to escape samsara altogether. A famous prayer from the Upanishads describes this state of moksha:

> From the unreal lead me to the real
> From darkness lead me to light
> From death lead me to immortality.
> Brihadaranyka Upanishad. 1 iii, 28

Moksha is described in many ways, as perfect peace and happiness, or as the soul losing itself in Brahman, or the bliss of union with God. It is a spiritual state of existence in which neither good nor bad deeds happen. Perfect peace and tranquillity fill the soul and deep wisdom and knowledge beyond human understanding is realised. It can be experienced but cannot be described:

> When all desires that rest in the heart are liberated shall a mortal man become immortal and attain Brahman.

It is described by Shankara, the great Indian philosopher, as 'pure being, existence and bliss.'

> Then in this deep serenity which arising up from this body, attains the highest light, reveals itself in its own true form; this is the Self (atman). So said he 'This is the immortal, this freedom from fear. This is Brahman. And the name of this Brahman is this Reality : and Reality is truth.'
> Chandogya Upanishad VIII, iii

Yoga

Most people in the West think yoga is a special form of exercise involving various postures and some meditation for general well being and health. This is a particular form of yoga known as Hatha yoga.

However, within Hinduism, yoga is much more than this. Yoga means unity and integration and is the means, methods and

Dandavati means undergoing punishment in this life in order to escape the consequences in future lives of any bad deeds one has done.

The photograph here shows a special pilgrimage route. Pilgrims prostrate themselves as they make their way up towards the sacred place. Acts such as this are believed to remove any bad karma and give the Hindu a chance to liberate his or her soul and reach the final goal of moksha.

discipline which bring union with a personal god, the supreme being or Brahman.

If a Hindu decides to make moksha their goal, they need to find a way in which material concerns and worldly ambition is considered to be less important than the spiritual path. That is why in India the way of the holy man as a sannyasin, sadhu, guru or swami is highly regarded.

The goal is to realise the true self (the atman) as identical with the ultimate reality of Brahman.

This goal is not easy to attain because human beings have strong desires and attachment to physical pleasures, material things and worldly concerns. Yoga requires strong commitment and great self discipline.

There are at least there recognised ways of doing this:
- karma yoga
- bhakti yoga
- jnana yoga.

Karma yoga

Karma yoga is the path of unselfish action. Doing one's daily work and particular duties of one's stage in life and caste selflessly, without any desire for reward or selfish gain, and using one's talents and fulfilling one's potential for the good of society, is considered to be the path of karma yoga.

Gandhi, who worked tirelessly and selflessly in campaigns for Indian independence and the upliftment of the untouchables, was seen as the ideal karma yogi.

Bhakti yoga

Bhakti yoga is the way of devotion to God. This is expressed in a loving relationship with a personal deity, in which the devotee remembers the god's name constantly and praises him or her through singing and chanting.

The devotee surrenders to their chosen lord completely and, with great emotion, experiences the peace and love of God. This enables them to take refuge in God and eventually reach moksha.

Jnana yoga

Jnana yoga is the way of knowledge and understanding. In this path, God is experienced as an impersonal force, and the path to self realisation is achieved through deep meditation and oneness with the supreme spirit Brahman.

This way enables one to pierce through the veil of illusion and ignorance and to gain insight into the true nature of things.

Raja yoga

Another form of yoga found in Indian scriptures is Raja yoga, or royal yoga. This is regarded by some Hindus as the highest form of yoga and the fulfilment of all the other three ways. This is a form of self control over both the senses and the mind, it involves deep contemplation of Brahman and, when success is achieved, the personality is transformed – freed from anger, lust, greed, envy and sadness.

The holy man in the photograph on the left is sitting in a yogic posture with his legs in the lotus position. He is an ascetic, who has renounced worldly comforts and chosen to develop his spiritual life.

A sign of extreme asceticism is an emaciated body, showing the ability to exist on very little food. A true holy man is dependent on gifts of food and other requirements from passers-by and visitors.

He may perform rituals for people who ask for special blessings and also spend a lot of time in meditation and chanting. The objects used in his puja and rituals are displayed in front of him.

Activities

Key Elements

1 How would you define the key concepts of samsara, karma and moksha?

2 How would a belief in karma and reincarnation affect a Hindu's outlook on life?

3 What are the differences and similarities between bhakti yoga, karma yoga, jnana yoga and raja yoga?

Think About It

4 What kinds of goals in life do you have?

5 Why does material success and wealth not always make people happy ?

6 What does the Hindu view of human life and destiny have in common with the attitude to life and destiny in the West?

Assignment

(a) What is meant by the two destinies of samsara and moksha?

(b) How does the law of karma affect reincarnation?

(c) Explain three ways in which moksha can be attained.

(d) "The belief in karma helps Hindus to accept any suffering they might experience in this life." Do you agree with this statement? Give reasons for your answer.

5

Scriptures

- The Vedas
- Popular Religious Literature

- The Puranas

These pilgrims have come to the Krishna temple at Jaipur to hear a special talk on the Bhagavad Gita from the famous Swami Srivatsa. The Bhagavad Gita is the most popular of all Hindu scriptures. In the photograph, temple priests are marking the foreheads of musicians with a tilaka of sandlewood paste.

The Vedas

The holy books of the Hindus are known as the Vedas. They are probably the oldest scriptures in the world which are still used today for ritual ceremonies and as a source of wisdom and truth.

It is very difficult to give a historical origin to these scriptures, but to Hindus the truths of the Vedas were first revealed by God at the beginning of human creation for the benefit of humankind, and they are timeless and eternal truths. The earliest part of the Vedas are thought to be the ancient hymns of the Aryans who composed hymns to their gods more than 3,500 years ago. They were learnt by heart and passed down by word of mouth through the priestly castes. These Vedas are called **shruti** texts because they are not believed to be of human origin but to have been revealed by Brahma the creator god to inspire the ancient seers. These wise men 'heard' the scriptures, which is why these first Hindu scriptures are shruti, which means 'heard'. Shruti expresses eternal truths and therefore has more authority than later scriptures, which are called **smriti**, 'remembered' truths

The word Veda means 'to know' and although they are of very ancient origin, they contain a wealth of knowledge about art, medicine, mathematics, science and philosophy.

The hymns of the Vedas are very beautiful; they describe the beauty of the dawn, the wondrous creation of the world and the journey of the soul through life, as well as scientific theories.

The Vedas consist of four books or collections of hymns:

- The **Rig Veda** is a collection of 1028 hymns written in an early form of Sanskrit, arranged in ten separate books (mandals) and used in the religious rituals of the Aryans.
- The **Sama Veda** deals with melodies and chants for sacred hymns to be sung at special sacrifices.
- The **Yajur Veda** is a kind of handbook for priests to guide them in the performance of rituals and sacrifices.
- The **Atharva Veda** contains 5977 verses of magical formulae and early scientific knowledge.

Passages from these Vedas form the basis for religious rituals performed by brahmin priests for both temple worship and domestic ceremonies such as rites of passage.

Questions

1 Why are the Vedas so important to Hindus?

2 What different kinds of knowledge do these scriptures contain?

3 What are the differences between shruti and smriti?

The Upanishads are another collection of scriptures which have a very special status: they reveal sacred truths in philosophical formulas. The word Upanishad is derived from the Sanskrit root 'shad' meaning to sit, to settle, or to approach, from the prefixes 'upa', meaning near and 'ni' meaning down. So the seeker of enlightenment approached a teacher, sat down at his feet and settled his mind and listened very carefully to his spiritual instructions. These teachings are therefore meant to be heard only by selected pupils who were dedicated to the pursuit of truth with their chosen guru or teacher.

These scriptures have survived in their present form since 200 BCE. There are thirteen major Upanishads and they express in their teachings a vast amount of spiritual insight into the self of man, the nature of Brahman, origin of the universe and the ultimate goal of liberation of the soul in moksha.

This is an orthodox brahmin priest reading scriptures and performing daily puja. The Vedas are written in Sanskrit and only the 'twice born' upper castes are considered pure enough to read them. It is the duty of Brahmins to know the scriptures and to explain them to others.

The upanishads are the basis for all Indian philosophy and many different schools of thought have emerged from them. They are as relevant and inspiring today as they were when they were first compiled and many famous western writers and philosophers have marvelled at the truths contained within them, but the truths they express are difficult to understand in a rational way, one needs to use intuition and imagination to appreciate them.

One version of a dialogue or conversation between a pupil and teacher in the Chandogya Upanishad has been translated as a story:

Once there lived a young boy called Svetaketu the son of Uddalaka Aruna. One day his father said, "My son, you are now twelve and the time has come for you to go and study the sacred teachings, for it is tradition in our family that everyone should study the Vedas and become a true brahmin."
When he was twenty-four Svetaketu returned home having studied all the Vedas. He was full of conceit and arrogantly thought he knew everything.
"Svetaketu," his father said. "You are conceited and arrogant and think yourself well read, but did you ever ask for that knowledge by which one hears what cannot be heard, sees that which cannot be seen and knows that which cannot be known?"
"Whatever is that teaching, sir?" the son enquired.
"Very well, my son. By knowing one lump of clay you know the essence of all things made of clay, the difference being only in name and form. By knowing
one nugget of gold you know the essence of all things made of gold, their difference being only name and form. In the same way, my son, through this knowledge you gain the essence of all knowledge."
"My venerable teachers could not have known of this for they would surely have passed it on to me. So could you dear father teach me?"
"Very well, my son. In the beginning there was one being, one without a second. Some people however, believe that in the beginning there was only non-Being, and that non-being gave birth to being."
"But how could this be? How could being arise from non-being?"
"No my son, it was pure being, one without second, that existed in the beginning. Pure Being thinking to itself 'May I become many, may I take form,' created light. Light thinking to itself, 'May I become many, may I take form,' created the waters. And the waters thinking to themselves 'May I become many, may I take form,' created the earth. In this way the whole universe was born from pure being. That being which is the subtlest essence of everything, the supreme reality, the self of all that exists, that art thou, Svetaketu."

Two of the most famous of Indian philosophers, Shankara and Ramanuja, have written many commentaries on the Upanishads and on the basis of these they have formed their own school of philosophical thought called Vedanta. There is a great deal of renewed interest in Vedanta in the West today.

This photograph shows a small, street shrine in which the scriptures (Vedas) are the object of devotion as well as the source of prayer and ritual. It is probably the place of a sadhu who has been left offerings of money to support himself in return for his teachings based on the scriptures.

The main occupation of Indian holy men, especially the gurus, sannyasins and swamis is to study and explain these teachings to those who seek spiritual guidance. Hindus might visit these swamis when they give audience in either holy cities and places of pilgrimage or in their own **ashrams**. Ashrams are retreat centres where people stay for a while to receive instruction and guidance from their guru. Some of these gurus and swamis are very popular and famous all over the world and receive a lot of attention from both Hindus and people from the West. In Britain today, swamis from India are welcomed at Hindu community centres and mandirs to give talks on Hindu scriptures.

Questions

1 Why do religious people put such faith and trust in sacred scriptures for answering life's questions?

2 Why do you think there are so many holy men in India, and why do so many people, including westerners, like to visit them and listen to their teachings?

Popular Religious Literature

The great Hindu epics the Mahabharata and the Ramayana belong to smriti scriptures. This means that the teachings are remembered rather than directly revealed to the listener, and these religious, moral and educational writings are known well by all Hindus.

The epics and stories were a way in which the ideals and values of the Hindu way of life, the religious beliefs and practices which guide Hindus through life, are expressed and made known to all Hindus regardless of social background and education. Although they may have originally been written in Sanskrit, in later centuries they were translated by a variety of Indian poets into regional languages so they could reach all Hindus. In the past they may have been recited at public ceremonies such as sacrifices, but today they are greatly enjoyed by Hindus through the modern media of cinema and television.

The Mahabharata

The Mahabharata was written about 900 BCE but was added to and amended over the next six or seven hundred years.

Its title means 'great epic of the Bharats' (Indian people sometimes refer to their country as Bharat). It is 200,000 verses long and is the world's longest poem. Hindus regard the great sage Vyasa as the author of this epic.

It deals with a power struggle between two royal families which represent the good forces (the Pandavas) and the evil forces (the Kauravas). The scene is the kingdom of the Kurus near modern day Delhi. The conflict arose because the right to the throne was in dispute. The father of the Kuru princes was the eldest brother but he was blind, and so his younger brother Pandu became king. However, King Pandu retired to the forest to live as a sannyasin, leaving the throne to his brother Dritharashtra.

Dritharashtra took his nephews into his household and treated them as his own sons. But his own sons became jealous of their cousins and resolved to murder them by setting fire to the house in which they were living. The five Pandhava brothers heard of the plot in time to escape to the forest where they lived in disguise far away from the capital. The greatest warrior and skilled archer amongst the Pandhavas was Arjuna, who won a beautiful princess as the prize in an archery contest.

Meanwhile, the blind king decided to give back half of his kingdom to the exiled Pandhava brothers. When the Kurus heard that the Pandhavas were still alive, and had a royal princess amongst them and ruled half of the kingdom from a new capital, they challenged their cousins to a gambling match.

The Pandhava brothers were given loaded dice and so were tricked by their Kauravas into losing their kingdom again. They were banished to the forest for thirteen years. When they

This carved stone frieze at Ellora tells the story of the Mahabharata.

returned to claim their rightful kingdom, their cousins refused to give it back. An enormous battle raged for eighteen years in which the Kuru brothers and their huge army were totally destroyed. The Pandavas ruled the kingdom righteously and then retired from worldly activities to the mountains of the Himalayas, to complete the fourth stage of life and prepare for final liberation of the soul and union with God.

The Bhagavad Gita

The word Gita means 'celestial song' and Bhagavad means 'Lord'. This section of the Mahabharata is the most famous and well known of all Hindu scriptures. It is included in the sixth book of the Mahabharata, although it was probably written much later, in the third century BCE. It has been the inspiration for many great thinkers well as ordinary folk, and has been called the jewel of ancient India's spiritual wisdom.

It tells the story of Arjuna preparing to fight his cousins in the terrible war. As the armies line up for battle at a place called Kurukshetra he is struck with horror at the prospect of killing his relatives. He orders his chariot to

withdraw and is then given advice by his charioteer, which is in fact Lord Krishna (an avatar of the god Vishnu) in disguise.

The special message of the Gita is that devotion to God, with complete surrender and trust, is the highest form of worship and a means to attain the highest goal of moksha. This is bhakti yoga.

He also teaches the way of karma yoga which is a way of fullfilling one's moral duties without desire for reward.

The Gita gives unique insight into the Hindu vision of the nature of God in chapter 11:

The great lord of power and yoga revealed to the son of Pandu his all highest form

A form with many a mouth and eye and countless marvellous aspects.

Many indeed were its divine adornments, many the celestial weapons raised on high. Garlands and celestial robes he wore, fragrance divine was his anointing.

Behold this God whose every mark spells wonder. The infinite facing in all directions

If in a bright heaven there should arise the light of a thousand suns then they would resemble this wondrous lord.

Arjuna then saw the whole wide universe in One converged.

There he saw the body of the God of gods yet divided out in many forms.

Then filled with amazement his hair standing on end Arjuna joined his hands in reverent greeting and bowed down before his lord.

This submission to a personal lord is the reason why the Bhagavad Gita is so popular. It is a yoga available to everyone, not just learned priests and sannyasins who have turned away from the world. The Gita offers a way to liberation through the love of God and so is open to all people regardless of age, caste, sex or social standing.

The Ramayana

The Ramayana is shorter than the Mahabharata and is believed to have been written by Valmiki between 200 BCE and 200 CE though it had been recited for many centuries before that.

The main message of this scripture is the triumph of good over evil and it is presented through the story of Rama and Sita. The story is very well known to Hindus, because it is recited at the festival of Divali (see page 80).

In the story there are many attractive characters – Rama, Sita, Lakshmana, Hanuman and Bharata. These display many good qualities

This is a stunning sight - a man dressed up to look like Hanuman. In the Ramayana, Hanuman is shown as a superhuman being who, although ruler of the monkey kingdom, has the ability to fly great distances and the strength to lift up mountains.

Hanuman is like an ancient version of Superman. He is utterly devoted to the princely God, Rama, and serves him with pure loyalty. He represents those qualities of faith, loyalty, service and strength. In this picture, the person is taking the role of Hanuman in a re-enactment of stories from the Ramayana.

which Hindus are encourage to develop. In this way the Ramayana has been used as a vehicle for moral and social teaching for two thousand years.

In particular, Rama is seen as the ideal husband, brother, son and king. Sita is seen as the ideal wife. Rama and Sita maintain their good qualities in spite of being the victims of cruelty and injustice and the various things they have to suffer in the course of the story.

The Ramayana is therefore a good example of the moral function of Hindu scripture. Hindus are encouraged to follow the examples of their heros and heroines as described in these stories. This is a very colourful and lively way to present moral teachings, and to illustrate the effect that these have on society.

Many of the great stories of Hindu literature are available in the form of comic strips, which are extremely popular. With accounts of kidnapping and battle, it is easy to see how the scriptures can be presented in this way. But there is always a moral point to be made and personal qualities to be displayed in each of these stories.

> ## Questions
>
> 1 Why are stories (including modern versions of these Hindu stories) a good way to express religious teachings?
>
> 2 Why do you think the Bhagavad Gita is such a popular scripture for Hindus?

The Puranas

The Puranas are a form of popular religious literature containing stories about the Hindu deities which help ordinary people relate to the main Hindu gods Vishnu, Shiva and Brahma.

They are later Indian scriptures, composed between the sixth and sixteenth centuries CE. In these stories the sages used the lives of saints and kings and historical events to explain the eternal teachings of Hinduism to the people.

The most widely known purana is the Bhagavad Purana which was composed for worshippers of Vishnu. There are hundreds of editions of this scripture, which glorifies Vishnu and his various avatars. The tenth book provides the biography of Krishna and is the most frequently read.

The stories show Krishna's powers as an avatar of Vishnu. Some Hindus regard the stories as true events, others simply use them to focus their loving devotion on Krishna.

> Thousands of years ago King Ugrasena ruled the city of Mathura in northern India. He was gentle by nature, but his son Kansa was a cruel tyrant, who even put his own father in prison. Kansa was warned by the gods that the eighth baby born to his sister Deviki would kill him, so he killed all of Deviki's babies, proving his wickedness.
>
> When she gave birth to her eighth son, Deviki's husband Vasudeva resolved to save him. Although the palace was heavily guarded, he made a miraculous escape to a village called Gokul where he left the baby child Krishna with a cowherd Nanda and his wife Yashoda.
>
> Kansa found out that the baby was still alive and sent various assassins to kill him. One of these assassins was Putana, whose speciality was poisoning children with her breast milk. However Krishna bit her and Putana bled to death.

The stories of Krishna's life reveal his miraculous feats in protecting the villagers from the disasters of floods, and wherever his influence was felt there was peace, harmony, goodness and happiness.

These stories both reveal the doctrine of bhakti, and also illustrate the belief that God takes many forms and intervenes in human affairs to ensure the well-being and progress of humankind and the protection of dharma.

Activities

Key Elements

1 Why are the Vedas considered by Hindus to be the most sacred of their scriptures and the other scriptures less so?

2 What are the main themes of the Mahabharata and Ramayana and why are these epics so popular with Hindus.

3 List all the different kinds of Hindu scriptures, and what makes them special.

Think About It

4 Why do some people place their trust in scriptures to guide them in their life and help them get closer to the truth?

5 Why do you think there are so many different kinds of scriptures in Hinduism?

Assignment

(a) What kinds of writings are found in the following Hindu scriptures: The Rig Veda, the Upanishads, the Epics?

(b) Explain the purpose of these scriptures within the Hindu tradition.

(c) "Scriptures can never be as important as personal experience in coming to know the reality of God."

Do you think a Hindu would agree or disagree with this statement? Give reasons for your answer. What is your own response to the statement?

6

Worship

- Puja
- Other Aspects of Worship
- The Mandir: temples and shrines
- Temple Worship
- The Purpose of Temples

Worship can take many forms, from elaborate rituals to a simple act of devotion or showing respect to a holy place, image or person. This photograph shows a family group of three generations of women who have visited Varanasi to meet with and receive blessings from this holy man. They have brought gifts and offerings for him. Next to him is the shrine he has set up.

To understand the nature and purpose of worship in Hinduism one has to appreciate the importance of ritual as way of expressing feelings, beliefs and relationship to the chosen deity or aspect of God. Although the Hindu concept of God is very abstract, in the purest sense of the impersonal absolute Brahman, many Hindus relate to God through the many different forms and images of Brahman in the popular deities and saints.

In response to the question 'Why do Hindus worship images and idols?' a Hindu priest explained to his questioner:

A believer sees in an image or idol what a non-believer cannot see. The immense faith and devotion that a person pours into an idol turns that idol into God for him. Perhaps it is only a stone to others, but to him it is God. We believe that God is omnipresent, that is, He is everywhere. If He is every where then surely He is in that idol too. Also the great sages of India knew that ordinary people would find it difficult to concentrate, so the image is used as a point of concentration to focus their minds when they meditate and communicate with God. So when we pray with the image in front of us this makes us aware of God's presence and we feel he is with us and we are able to ask him to bless us with the good things in life.

Images on the tower of the temple of Kumbhewara.

Shrines are made to fit anywhere. This one is on the typical steps (or ghats) that are found alongside the River Ganges. The shrine has been made to fit into the architecture. In this photograph you can also see the dwelling place of someone who is living alongside it.

The chosen deity is regarded as an honoured guest in the home and as the resident royalty in temples and shrines. Throughout India, in every possible place – shops, cafes, taxis, lorry cabs, roundabouts, and inside banyan trees – shrines are found indicating the reality of the divine presence dwelling in every aspect of life. This sometimes seems strange to non-Hindus, who find it difficult to visualise the nature of God and tend to separate the sacred aspects of life from the ordinary or profane. However, the actions performed by Hindus in their homes and temple to show their devotion to God can be understood in very simple terms as well as with more complex meaning.

Puja

Puja is the nearest word in Hinduism to the word 'worship'. It actually means paying respects or homage to God through various actions which express the wish to please one's chosen deity and offer service to them and hope for the blessing of God in return for this act of devotion. The same basic rituals of puja are performed at the shrine in the home as well as in the temple, except that one is more simple and the other more elaborate and dramatic. It is an individual act of devotion and each person performs it is his or her own way.

Puja in the home

In every Hindu home there is a place set aside for a small shrine to their chosen and favourite family deity, in a small room or a specially fitted cupboard or shelf. Puja is usually performed by women, although it can involve the whole family, and takes place every morning and evening.

Objects found on a shrine in the home.

The objects found on a shrine would include images and pictures of the gods and goddesses. The items used in puja are:

- A small (usually copper) vessel containing water from the holy river Ganges
- Red kum-kum powder, yellow tumeric powder, sandlewood paste
- Flowers and leaves
- Food offering of sweetmeats and fresh fruit
- Incense
- A small ghee lamp (usually a small dish with a cotton wool wick placed in ghee or clarified butter)
- An arti lamp
- A small bell.

Puja in the home. On this shrine you can see items used for puja. Try to match them up with the list given above. Notice the various images and pictures of deities and one or two members of the family who have died.

The actions of puja and their meaning

1 Before puja in the home, those taking part will bathe and dress in clean clothes. This shows respect and the desire to clean both body and soul and to clear away ignorance.

2 The deity is invited to be present in the image by special prayers and ringing the bell.

3 The deity is offered a special seat and welcomed like an honoured guest, and a water offering made in a similar way.

4 The deities are given a ceremonial bath using panchamrit, a mixture of milk, yoghurt, sugar, honey and butter. The image is washed with clean water and dried. It is given fresh clothes, specially made to fit the image. Sometimes a sacred thread is placed on it.

5 Tumeric powder, red kum-kum powder, sandalwood paste and rice is put on each deity. Sandalwood is known to have a calming effect so this action enables the worshipper to feel calm and relaxed.

6 Brightly coloured, sweet-smelling flowers are laid before the figures or hung over them as garlands. The offering of flowers should be done in a particular way. Firstly the five fingers of the right hand are used to pick up the flower gently, then the fingers are turned upward with the flower, which is offered at the deity's feet. The flowers represent worldly desires and the offering of flowers shows the willingness to get rid of one's desires and express love and devotion for the deity.

7 Incense sticks, and sometimes camphor, are lit to create a fragrant atmosphere. Fragrant oils, representing the destruction of selfish desires, may be burnt.

8 Then a small ghee lamp is lit and waved before the deity.

9 Fruits and food are ceremonially offered to the deity to thank God for the bounty given by him to all beings. Coconut and betel leaves might be arranged around the deity.

10 Then the **arti** ceremony is performed. A special arti lamp, containing five cotton wool wicks dipped in purified butter, is lit. The number five represents the five elements of earth, air, wind, water and fire. This lamp is rotated around the deity while a small bell is rung. Then the devotees symbolically accept the light and blessing of god by passing their hands over the flame and then over their head. This action represents the desire to seek enlightenment and to destroy the darkness of ignorance and receive the light of knowledge.

This is a shrine to Krishna. He is shown with a black face (Krishna means 'dark'). Notice the food offerings that have been placed in front of the shrine as part of the celebrations for the festival of Divali.

So all the actions of puja are performed for the specific purpose of bringing the presence of the deity in to the home and to help the worshipper develop a good state of mind, with loving feelings towards God and all beings, to concentrate on the inner spiritual self and seek wisdom and understanding.

Two important prayers or mantras are recited during puja:

The arti prayer

O Lord of the universe, Supreme Soul, Dispeller of sorrow, hail to you. Your rule of righteousness be established everywhere, it is you who banishes in an instant the troubles of your devotees. May your kingdom of virtue reign supreme. Whoever meditates upon you receives your grace. The worries of his mind disappear: his home is blessed with peace, happiness and plenty and all his bodily pains vanish.

Destroy our base desires and wipe out our sins, increase our faith and devotion. May we serve you and your devotees.

The Gayatri mantra

Om Bhur swah. Tatsavitur varenyam bhargo devasya dhimahi, dhio yo nah prachodayat.

The Protector, Who is the basis of life of the whole universe and who is self existent.
Who is free from all pains and Whose contact frees the souls from all troubles
pervades this multi-formed universe and sustains all.
He is the Creator and Energiser of the whole universe, the Giver of all happiness,
Worthy of acceptance, the most Excellent.
Pure and Purifier.
That very God. Let us embrace so that God may direct our minds.

These women pilgrims have made a shrine on the banks of the Ganges. You can see some of the usual objects used for puja, including a bowl for the sacred water and an arti lamp. The women have brought with them a basket with leaves and lamps to make special divas to float in the river at sunrise.

Activities

Key Elements

1 What are the main actions performed in puja?

2 Explain the meaning and purpose of puja in the home and in the temple.

3 How do the actions performed during puja show that Hindus regard the deity as an honoured guest in the home?

Think About It

4 Why do you think some religious people like to worship God in their home and others prefer to go to a special place, like a temple or church, for worship?

Other Aspects of Worship

BHAKTI

While puja is paying one's respects to God, bhakti is a deep, intense and personal devotion to God. This is a special form of worship: the expression of love in an emotional way, and the complete surrender to one's personal Lord. Bhakti is sometimes expressed in devotional worship of a congregational kind (e.g. kirtan). Devotees gather in groups and sing **bhajans** (hymns) written by famous poets and saints. There has been a long tradition of bhakti worship in India and some modern movements, such as Krishna Consciousness, express this in their chanting and devotional worship.

HAVAN

This is a fire sacrifice which is performed on special occasions usually at the temple. It was the central act of ancient Vedic ritual. The fire is the god Agni. Offerings of rice and ghee are made to the fire. The fire is said to be the tongue of the gods, by means of which they consume the offerings. Since there are no food offerings to be shared, the bystanders participate in the ritual by receiving the ash.

YAJNA

This is a form of public worship in which people gather together to worship God and express their intention to be selfless and dedicated in their service to the community. It expresses the sacrifice of personal desires and of the ego.

This shrine is in a specially made building in the garden of the house of a wealthy brahmin family. On this occasion they have a special visiting priest. He is sitting on the right and wearing white. A member of the family is attending to the shrine, while the others wait for puja.

The Mandir: Temples and Shrines in India

India is sometimes called the land of temples as they are situated everywhere, in places associated with appearances of the gods, or where special miracles may have taken place. Shrines are like miniature temples and are found in many different forms in every village and along the roadside. The mandir is often the most prominent building in the village, made of brick and brightly painted and decorated with images of the gods. In small towns, especially those alongside a river, the temple would be placed near the edge of the river with steps reaching down into the water.

The Hindu temple or **mandir** is a symbol with many meanings. It is intended to be a special place for the encounter between the worshipper and the divine, a place where the divine and human can meet. They are not meeting places for a congregation, but for the individual worshipper or small group. The idea is to leave the busy world behind as you go through the gateway to approach the inner shrine and to seek the truth within you. Just as with any religious building, it is designed to help produce a certain state of mind. The external surroundings remind the worshipper of the special nature and qualities of their god. It is a way of creating a kind of divine realm or a kind of heaven on earth.

The Hindu temple is a symbol of the universe, and the different designs and plans correspond to the regions of the earth, sky and the homes of the various gods. It is a microcosm of the universe, with the animal kingdom at the base working up through the human realms to the divine.

The design of Hindu temples

In Hindu mythology, mountains are the dwelling places of the gods. In the Himalayas, Kailasha (or Mount Meru) is both the centre of the world and the home of Shiva and Parvati. So the basic shape of a temple is meant to be like a mountain and to provide the most beautiful and splendid palace for the gods, who are like divine royalty dwelling in their mansions on earth.

There is a difference of style in the shape and layout of temples in the north and south of India but there are some basic features which all temples have.

The basic purpose of the mandir is to house the deities, so the centre or focus of the whole building is the inner sanctum where the image or **murti** of the deity is installed. This place is called the **garbha-griha**, which means 'womb house', and directly above this is the **shikhara**, a tower-like structure or spire. The whole of the inner shrine is called the **vimana** and the shikhara symbolises the sacredness of this place. It also represents the highest level of the mind or liberation (moksha), and the tower leads the eye upwards towards liberation.

Devotees used to come to worship and stand in front of the shrine. In the course of time this space in front of the shrine was cleared and raised to make a platform where people could come together. Eventually this space was made into a hallway with a roof and pillars and was called a **mandapa**. At first, the mandapa was separated from the vimana, but they became joined by an series of steps leading down into the main shrine room. Also a covered porch or entrance hall was added with steps leading up to the mandapa.

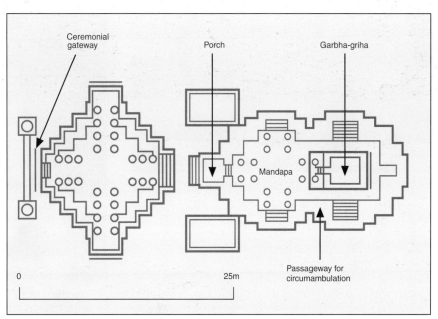

This is the plan of a traditional Hindu temple.

In Britain, the Hindu community have put a great deal of effort and commitment into creating new mandirs. At first they converted existing buildings, but in the last ten years some purpose-build temples have been made. The most famous of these is the Swami Narayan temple in Neasden, London, which is the largest outside India.

The photo on the right shows a view of that temple from the side.

The photograph below shows the elaborate Shikhara of a famous Shaivite temple in Bombay. This temple is considered to be one of the five 'jyotirlingas' in the state of Maharashtra where Shiva is worshipped.

sanctum so that the worshippers can circumambulate the deity. The outside of the temple may have many elaborate decorations showing the stories of the gods and events from the great epics, such as the Mahabharata.

The style of temples in the south of India is different from this basic structure. Here the most prominent feature is not the Shikhara but the **gopuram**, which are towers or large gateways in the outer walls.

The temple of Kumbakonam. This style of temple is typical of Southern India.

At the entrance to the temple there is a separate shrine which houses the guardian of the deity, which is usually the vehicle of the deity (e.g. Nandi the bull for Shiva, and Garuda the eagle for Vishnu). In large temples there are other shrines to the consorts of the deities around the mandapa or front entrance hall. Also many temples have a circular path around the inner

Worship in Hindu temples

A group of temple musicians offering puja to Krishna at a shrine in Vrindaban. How can you tell they are musicians? Notice the items on the tray. Notice the small arti lamp, incense holder and flowers.

When Hindus visit a temple it will be for a special purpose or intention or a festival occasion. They will perform their own individual puja or join in congregational worship if that is going on. The worshipper has to be in a state of ritual purity in order to receive the divine blessings. This is why women in menstruation and some of the lower castes are often barred from entering temples. Men and women wear traditional dress rather than western clothes. They remove their shoes on entering, ring the bell near the entrance and then perform some or all of the following ritual actions:

Prostration before the chosen deity: the devotee lies flat on his stomach with his arms stretched over his head and palms together in a gesture of humility and desire to serve God.

Circumambulation of the temple: walking around the temple or the inner walkway three times, with the temple on their right side (a traditional mark of respect).

Offerings of flowers and fruit. A coconut is often offered, as it is a symbol of the pure inner self within a tough outer shell. This might be given to the temple priest who will break the shell, tear the tuft and pour the pure milk over the murti.

Arti might be performed and other acts of puja as well as some quiet meditation or reading of sacred scriptures.

The most important part of the temple worship is **darshan** (seeing the image in the garba griha). The room is dark like a mountain cave and the priest reveals the image by the light of the flame in the tray. The worshippers pass their right hands over the flame and make offerings of flowers, fruit and a donation to the priest. Then each worshipper is given a flower or garland from the shrine as a token of God's grace, or in some temples given some food to eat. This food is called **prashad** which means 'God's grace, favour or kindness'.

In this way the temple worship is a means of changing the devotee's attitude towards life. The aim is to withdraw attention from the outside world and look into the inner world of one's self and one's divine nature and then return to the world spiritually refreshed.

Question

- In what way does the design of a temple express religious beliefs?

The installing of murtis in the temple

The presence of god is symbolised by the images inside the temple. In the temples of Shiva this is often the linga, in others, images of the gods and goddesses in anthropomorphic or human-like form. These images are called **murtis**.

There is a special ceremony for installing the deities in a new temple called Prana Pratishta, which means breathing into the image the life-giving energy of the deity. The murti can then become a channel for divine blessings. The murtis are seen as containing part of the nature of the deity, but are not identical with the deity, so they can be a focus for devotion. The murti is a temporary form into which the divine energy can descend when the worshippers invite the deity to dwell in their hearts.

The image is a representation of the deity and is treated like royalty in a palace. The rituals which take place as part of the daily life in the temple revolve around the daily need of the deities; so they are dressed, bathed and garlanded, given food offerings and put to rest.

The purpose of temples in India and in Britain

There are so many wonderful Hindu temples in India that they are testimony to the central importance of the Hindu faith in shaping the culture of India. As well as their obvious religious purpose for worship, temples have from ancient times met other needs too. Some are important centres of learning and research, other specialise in providing help to the needy through charitable works, others have given medical care and support. They always come into their own at festival times when the elaborate public processions are organised from them so they can galvanise the community into action.

There are over one million Hindus living in Britain today, most of whom have come from the Punjab or Gujarat or possibly from the Asian community in East Africa. There are now quite sizeable Hindu communities in most of the major cities and during the last ten years several new temples have been built and existing ones improved.

These temples are very important for the

The marriage of the gods. This is part of a ceremony held in a mandir in Preston. When a new mandir is opened, a special ceremony is performed to install the murtis in the temple. This is a way of making the mandir a sacred place in which the living presence of the deity can exist.

A temple, set in the midst of a village in the state of Maharashtra, about 100kms east of the pilgrims' town of Paithan. The brightly coloured towers contrast sharply with the humble dwellings and rural surroundings.

Hindu community in Britain, as they serve a social, cultural and religious purpose. They provide a focus for the community to meet and strengthen social and cultural bonds as a minority community in a western culture.

Since many British Hindus are not able to perform elaborate puja at home, the temple is especially important for preserving religious traditions and instructing the younger generation in the Hindu culture.

In Britain there is much more emphasis on congregational worship than in India. Hindus will travel some distance to attend these services, as it gives them a valuable chance to meet up with other Hindu families as well as to engage in worship.

As the Hindu communities have become more established they have improved and developed their temples and been able to pay for the full-time services of temple priests. In this way, they are able to maintain and preserve

their cultural traditions, social bonds with other Hindus, and their religious rituals through their own temples in Britain.

Most Hindu mandirs in Britain have developed a community centre alongside the temple in which a variety of activities take place.

These may include:

- language classes in Gujarati

- cultural activities and classes in music and Indian dance

- youth clubs

- senior citizens' luncheons

- special talks and lectures from visiting holy men (swamis)

- weddings

Activities

Key Elements

1 Name all the main features of a Hindu mandir and describe their purpose.

2 What do Hindus understand to be the purpose of the murtis in a mandir?

3 Why is the temple likely to be the most elaborate and prominent feature of an Indian village?

Think About It

4 The lines on the palm of a hand are said to be a map of the life of that person, in that way it is a microcosm (miniature representation) of a much larger and more complex reality. Can you think of any other examples of microcosms? How can it apply to a Hindu mandir which has been described as a microcosm of the universe?

5 How might offering daily puja affect a Hindu's attitude to the day ahead and the rest of their daily life?

6 'Hinduism is a religion of the home rather than the temple.' Do you agree with this view? Give reasons for your answer, showing that you have considered more than one point of view.

Assignments

1 Visit a Hindu temple and take the opportunity to observe puja and find out the meaning of the chanting and the purpose of the actions performed.

2 'The Hindu mandir in Britain is essential to the preservation of Hindu culture in this country.' How far do you agree with this statement? Give reasons for your answer, showing that you have considered more than one point of view.

7

Festivals

- Maha Shrivratri
- Janmashtami - Krishna's Birthday
- Holi
- Raksha Bandan
- Navaratri, Durga Puja, Dusserah
- Divali

Hindu festivals can be quite dramatic. These people are celebrating the festival of Holi in a temple (see page 76).

Festivals are celebrated in every culture and there are common themes and experiences which everyone can relate to. Some festivals happen at key points in the year, according to the seasons, giving beginnings and endings to the year and expressing the feelings of hope and fulfilment which go with Spring and Autumn in spring and harvest festivals.

Festivals can be specifically religious and based on special events or religious teachings, reminding people of their faith and providing an opportunity to express their devotion and renew their commitment. They are times when families and communities gather together to enjoy each other's company, as well as remember and recollect the values and beliefs that they hold in common. Festivals can also link a community with the past, by recollecting important historical events which have influenced their present situation.

They provide opportunities for domestic creativity in the special foods and decorations which are produced at these times and the music, plays and dancing which are saved for these festival occasions. So festivals serve many purposes and the fact that festivals have continued throughout the ages shows how important they are, even if they are taken for granted.

- They have a social function in bringing families and communities together, and reminding them of their common bonds.
- They serve a religious and cultural function, as festivals are often rooted in the religious beliefs and practices and therefore educate the younger generations in the teachings and practices of the faith.
- They have an emotional and psychological function in providing the opportunity to reflect on one's life and experience the feelings of joy and suffering which are an inevitable part of one's own life, as well as a shared experience with the community.

Hinduism has a variety of festivals, some clearly related to seasonal changes, others to particular deities. In India, some festivals are marked by public processions (called **ratha-yatra,** chariot procession) from the temple through the streets. Images of the deities are specially made from clay wood or cow dung and are dressed in ceremonial robes, garlands and crowns. (The temple murtis themselves are consecrated and should not be used for this purpose.) The images of the deities are placed on decorated carts or lorries which go on parade throughout the village, town or city together with elephants in regalia, street music, dancing and singing. The procession passes devotees' dwelling places and they can offer puja as it goes by. A famous procession takes place from Jagannath temple at Puri and the special chariot for the deity is so massive that this is where the word 'juggernaut' comes from. At the end of the festival the images of the deities are ceremoniously thrown into the nearest river.

> ## Questions
>
> 1 Why do you think festivals are found in every culture in the world?
>
> 2 Can you distinguish between the social and the religious aspects of festivals? Explain each aspect in your own words.

The procession of Maharumbhasan Tanthavur from the temple. This is a typical procession where images of a deity are paraded round the locality. In this picture you can see scaffolding on the temple. This is part of the festival when people engage in cleaning the murtis and sculptures of the deities. Can you see the canopy and the coconut? The coconut is a symbol of the pure self inside the coarse outer body, and they are therefore often used as offerings to the deities.

Maha Shrivratri

In the Hindu month of Magha (January/February) there is a winter festival to Shiva. It is a deeply religious festival, especially for devotees of Shiva. It is thought of as the anniversary of his marriage to the goddess Parvati, and the time when his devotees remember the time he saved humanity from disaster by drinking a draught of poison which a demon was planning to use to kill the population of the world.

The day is a fast until the late afternoon, when a special puja is offered to Shiva. Then, when the fast is over, only certain foods are allowed. Unmarried women sometimes fast and keep a vigil through the night in the hope that Shiva will find them husbands. Worship is offered to Shiva between midnight and sunrise. It takes the form of repeating his name and placing flowers and grain on his image. The next day everyone celebrates with a feast.

Celebrating Maha Shrivratri in Leicester. This Hindu couple are purifying the Shiva lingum with milk, yoghurt and water.

Janmashtami

This celebrates Krishna's birthday and takes place in the Hindu month of Sravana (August). It is believed that Krishna was born at midnight, so many Hindus stay up all night to keep a vigil. Often a cot is placed on the shrine in the temple and people place small gifts for the infant. The story of Krishna's birth and dramatic escape from a cruel king is retold. Krishna devotees will stay up all night singing bhajans to show their love and devotion for Krishna.

This is a special shrine made for the festival of Janmashtami. The young Hindu boy is standing in front of Krishna's cradle, while the sadhu looks on.

Holi

This is a seasonal festival, celebrating the coming of Spring with the joys and hope for a year of abundance in nature and happiness in family relationships and friendships. It is one of the most joyful festivals, and is a time for fun as much as religious devotion. It is celebrated on the full moon of the Hindu month of Phalguna (February) at the start of India's hot season.

The Holi festival at Vrindaban. This photo conveys the happy mood of Holi, in which families take time out to enjoy having fun, even if they do get covered with water and coloured powders!

What do Hindus do at Holi?

There is a custom of lighting a bonfire on the eve of Holi and roasting grains, pop corn, chick peas and coconut in the fire as offerings to the gods, which are later shared out as prashad. These roasted grains are called Holuk, giving Holi its name (as well as the story of Holika which is linked with this festival).

· When the fire is blazing, people walk around it carrying their children and babies and making offerings of grains to the fire.

It is known as the festival of colour because it is celebrated with coloured powders and water which everyone throws at each other with lots of fun and laughter. This is a festival in which one is allowed to break some of the usual rules of behaviour, so there is a lot of teasing as people wear their old clothes, forget all barriers of caste and rank and throw coloured water and bright powders at each other. Students chase their teachers down the streets and workers spray their bosses with powder. In the afternoon people go home for a bath, visit family and friends and exchange sweets and good wishes.

In Britain is it is not possible to have a public holiday and such exuberant celebrations in the streets, but Hindus do gather together at their community centre or sometimes a nearby park and have a bonfire and party.

Stories told at Holi express the theme of goodness overcoming evil, the most significant one being that of Holika and Prahlad.

> The was a tyrant of a king called Hiranyakashipu who demanded that everyone should worship him, as he considered himself to be the lord of the universe, but his son Prahlad would only worship Vishnu. The king tried to force his son to bow down to him, but Prahlad resisted. The king set out to kill him, persuading his sister Holika to carry Prahlad into the flames of a furnace. She had been promised by her brother that she had a gift from the gods that would save her from being burnt. But this promise did not work and she was burned in the flames, but her brother who was loyal to God was miraculously saved.

This story reminds Hindus of the rewards of loyalty and devotion to God and how this faith can overcome evil.

Other Holi stories focus on Krishna as a young cowherd who enchanted the milkmaids with the music of his flute. Songs and dances tell of the love between Krishna and his lover Radha. The total self surrender of Radha to her lord reminds Hindus of the need to surrender themselves in devotion to God.

The meaning of Holi

The significance of the colours of Holi are that they express delight at the beauty of the created world, so the religious meaning of this festival is to express the happiness of being alive and to remove barriers of hatred and bitterness which cause unhappiness between people.

It also reminds Hindus of the importance of loyalty and devotion to God and the belief that goodness can overcome evil.

The social meaning of the festival is that it celebrates togetherness and unites in friendship all people, regardless of caste and social background.

This festival helps to renew bonds of friendship and unity among families and the community.

This is an effigy of Holika which has been placed on the ghats near the River Ganges. Later it will be burnt in a bonfire for Holi celebrations to symbolise the destruction of evil forces and the triumph of goodness. In the story of Holika, she perished in the flames because she tried to deceive the gods.

Activities

Key Elements

1 What time of year is celebrated at Holi?

2 What is the meaning behind all the things that Hindus do during Holi?

3 In what way is Holi celebrated differently in Britain, compared with India?

Think About It

4 Do you think that Holi is a social get together rather than a religious festival? Give your reasons.

Raksha Bandan

This is celebrated on the day of full moon in the month of Shravan (August). It continues to grow in popularity as a festival, especially among British Hindus, as it provides a chance to strengthen bonds with family living in India.

It is celebrated in the home rather than the temple and all women, both young girls and adults, rise early and, before eating, tie a silk thread with a bright shiny decoration around the right wrist of each of their brothers. They then give their brothers some sweet meats and occasionally the girls receive a sari.

The thread is called a **raksha** or a rakhi, which means 'protection'. Bandhan means 'to tie'. Thus it is a tie of protection and symbolises the bonds of loyalty and friendship.

Navaratri, Durga Puja and Dusserah

This Hindu boy and girl live in Britain. You can see the delight and pleasure in the girl's face as she ties the rakhi around her brother's wrist. It is a valuable opportunity to show love and affection rather than fighting and squabbling.

In India, stalls appear everywhere selling rakhis and in Britain brothers receive them as gifts through the post, and proudly display them to show how much they are loved by their sisters. Friends also exchange these friendship bands.

The tradition of tying a special thread is an ancient one in India. It is used in the sacred thread ceremony and when the guru ties the band around his disciple's wrist to show the bond of love and trust between teacher and pupil. So Raksha Bandha shows the duty of the brother to protect his sister from trouble and danger.

Women without brothers tie the rakhi on men who can then regard them as sisters. It shows the respect of the man for the woman and is a universal symbol of brotherhood and sisterhood.

This festival falls in the Hindu month of Ashwin, during the Autumn. It is a very special festival, which is celebrated all over India, because it celebrates the feminine aspect of the goddess, Shakti. This word means 'cosmic energy' - the energy which makes the universe alive. Navaratri means 'nine days' and so devotion to the goddess continues for nine nights, then on the tenth day (the victory day, or Dusserah) the victory of Rama over the demon Ravanna is celebrated.

During this festival the goddess is worshipped in some form. For example, Durga Puja in West Bengal or the mother goddess (Mataji) in Gujarat. The festival celebrates the power of the goddess to fight evil and protect people. So special puja is given to the goddesses of Lakshmi, Durga, Saraswati and Kali.

In some households, a special shrine is made for the image of the goddess and puja is performed twice a day. An oil lamp is lit and kept burning for nine days. Each day, garlands of flowers are hung above the image.

In West Bengal, during their festival of Durga Puja, special Durga images are made and paraded through the streets.

This festival is famous for the special dances which are performed by the women in the evening at the mandir. They are called garba (dance circles) and danga ras (stick dance). It is said that the women are like the gopis who danced all night with their beloved Krishna, and sometimes young girls are dressed up and honoured as if they were the goddesses.

In Britain this festival is very important to Hindus from Gujarat and sometimes special halls are hired to make sure there is room for all the dancing.

In some parts of India, the tenth day (Dusserah) is celebrated with public gatherings and fireworks, in which large figures of the demon Ravanna, made from bamboo and paper, are eventually blown up or set on fire to show the overcoming of evil by the gods.

The women dance around a special shrine to the goddess, called a garbo. A picture of a different goddess is on each side of the box, which is decorated with lights and tinsel. During the evenings, many offerings and an arti ceremony is made before the shrine.

The photo on the left shows the burning of an image of Ravanna in Leicester.

Activities

Key Elements

1 What are the following features of Navaratri – Durga puja; garba; dandya ras; garbo?

2 How is the message of good overcoming evil shown at this festival?

Think About It

3 Why do you think it is important to have a festival especially for the goddess and why is this festival popular with women?

Divali

This is the best known festival of all. It begins at the dark end of one month, Asvina (October) and the new moon at the beginning of the next month, Karttik. The name of the festival means 'cluster of lights' and refers to the clay lamps which are placed inside and outside every home and temple. They relate to the story of Rama and Sita, who needed a row of lights to guide them on their homeward journey to Adyodhya after their victory over the demon king Ravanna.

In Britain and in India, Hindus decorate homes and public buildings with many brightly coloured lights. There is a special house cleaning, and pavement drawings, called rangoli patterns, are made with brightly coloured chalks. New clothes are worn and presents are given out.

Divali also marks the beginning of the new year for Hindus, so it is regarded as a good day to sort out business accounts, settle all debts and start new accounts. There is a special puja in the mandir for business men who make offerings to Ganesha for good luck. There is also special puga for Lakshmi, the goddess of wealth. Some Hindu children believe that the goddess Lakshmi, guided by the lamps, visits the homes of good children and leaves gifts for them.

These people are shaping a figure out of mud and cow dung for the festival of Divali. It is being prepared in the mandipa of the temple using coloured powders.

Hindus in Britain say that Divali is their Christmas, because there is plenty of special food, exchange of presents and greetings cards.

The religious meaning of Divali is again the triumph of good over evil, the coming of light or wisdom into the darkness of evil and ignorance and the opportunity to make a new start in all aspects of life.

The story of Rama and Sita in the Ramayana is associated with Divali and is sometimes re-enacted in plays and pageants.

Business people opening their new account books at Divali.

The Story of Divali

Many years ago in India there lived a king called Dasratha, who rules over the kingdom of Ayodhya. He had three wives and four sons. The eldest son Rama was heir to the throne but was also the god Vishnu in human form. Queen Kaikeyi, Dasratha's favourite wife, was jealous because Rama was to become king but she wanted her son to inherit the kingdom. So she told her husband lies about Rama with the result that Dasratha banished Rama from his kingdom and sent him into exile for fourteen years. Rama had a beautiful wife, Sita, who insisted on going into exile with him, together with his brother Lakshmana. They lived in the forest, but one day, while Rama and Lakshmana were out hunting, the demon king of Ravanna changed himself into a deer and tricked Sita into leaving her protected place in the forest. Then he kidnapped her and took her away to the island of Sri Lanka. When the brothers found out what had happened, they were determined to rescue Sita. Hanuman the monkey king, who was utterly devoted to Rama, came to their aid. With all the monkeys in the forest, they got together an army and built a bridge over the sea to Lanka with their own bodies. After ten days of fierce fighting, they finally killed the demon Ravanna. Sita was reunited with her husband and they returned to Ayodhya now that their exile was over. The people of the kingdom lit divas all along the way so that they could find their way back home.

Activities

Key Elements

1 In which Hindu month are the following festivals celebrated: Holi, Raksha Bandan; Navaratri, Shrivratri; Divali; Janmashtami?

2 What is the religious message of each of these festivals?

Think About It

3 What can Hindu children find out about their religion from these festivals?

4 What do you think is the most important function of festivals for the Hindu community both in India and in Britain?

Assignment

Choose one of these festivals and find out more details about how it is celebrated in either India or Britain.

Imagine you are invited to attend this with a Hindu friend. Write a letter to your friend describing your experience.

Pilgrimage

- Why do Hindus go on Pilgrimage?
- Places of Pilgrimage

- What Hindus do on Pilgrimage

Sadhus and pilgrims take part in ritual bathing during the Kumba Mela at Hardwar.

Throughout history people have been attracted to sacred places and visited them to soak up the atmosphere and draw on their spiritual power. This is the origin of the notion of pilgrimage which means travelling to a sacred place.

India is renowned for its many holy places and millions of Hindus from within India and throughout the world visit them. While some religious acts are considered to be essential to Hindu practice, pilgrimage is regarded as highly desirable but optional. It is very popular in India and many tour operators specialise in this.

The word for pilgrimage in Hinduism is Yatra. It is a religious act performed to experience the spiritual atmosphere of a place and some spiritual benefit or blessing. Going on pilgrimage is not like going on holiday, it is meant to involve some self-sacrifice and physical hardship, because it is an attempt to concentrate on one's spiritual life and leave the material world behind.

Why do Hindus go on Pilgrimage?

Hindus go on Yatra as a personal act of thanksgiving and as an expression of faith.

Since water is a natural cleansing agent and essential to life, a pool or river in a sacred place is regarded as a means of washing away sins and entering into a new life. The seven sacred rivers of India are all associated with pilgrimage. All the bad karma from previous misdeeds in this and previous lives can be washed away. If the reason for going on pilgrimage is to make amends for some sin or misdeed, then the pilgrim will choose to make their pilgrimage arduous and testing, as a kind of penance. The highest motive for going on pilgrimage is to seek spiritual liberation or moksha. This religious journey provides a unique opportunity to engage in some soul searching and deep contemplation of the real purpose of life.

Some Hindus have a particular reason for going on pilgrimage. They might be seeking to ask the deity of that place to cure them of an illness, or it might be for the fulfilment of a vow or promise they may have made to their chosen deity when seeking some favour or blessing.

Some pilgrims who visit the River Ganges live by its banks, eating, sleeping, washing, bathing and praying. The river is believed to purify and cleanse body, mind and soul.

This group of women, both young and old, have gathered together by the banks of the River Ganges to sing bhajans (sacred songs) and enjoy each other's company. Although pilgrimage can be quite arduous, there is also a joyous side, when both men and women gather together and share experiences. Along the banks of the Ganges there are special ashrams (places to stay) for people of various towns and villages in India, so that they can visit every year and have accommodation set aside for them.

Places of pilgrimage

Since water is a sacred symbol, most of the most famous holy places are on India's mighty rivers, Varanasi or Benares being the most famous.

The River Ganges flows from the Himalayas in the north right across the Deccan plain, finally flowing out into the ocean at the Bay of Bengal. Its life-giving properties and importance for the area are self evident.

The origins of the Ganges are expressed mythologically. Ganga, the river goddess, is said to have been reluctant to come down to earth because her immense power would be too destructive. She only agreed to come when Shiva, who lives in the Himalayas, agreed to tie her down by using the locks of his hair.

These photographs show the many temples and ashrams which line the banks of the River Ganges at Varanasi. Each state has its own special ashram where pilgrims can stay free of charge.
The many umbrellas or parasols mark the resting places of holy men who live by the river.
The steps leading down to the river are called ghats. Pilgrims walk down these into the river to bathe and perform puja.

Varanasi is particularly associated with rites for the dead. Many people go to the banks of the river to die and even ask to be lowered into the water so they can be in contact with it as they come to the end of their lives. They are cremated on its banks, and the ashes of those who die elsewhere may be sent to the Ganges or some other river.

Other places of pilgrimage on rivers include Allahabad, on the confluence of the Ganges and Jumna rivers. Also, Gangotri, Badrinath, Rishikesh and Hardwar, on the upper reaches of the Ganges, which attract many pilgrims despite the hardships of walking in the cold Himalayas. Gangotri is the source of the river, high up in the Himalayas, and the journey there is particularly arduous.

Hindus believe that, if a dying person sips the water from the source of the River Ganges, their soul will be liberated. Therefore, at certain times of the year, the sick and dying are carried on stretchers up to this special place, where there are many shrines and dwelling places for sadhus and ascetics.

These Sadhus are on a pilgrimage to Badrinath. They are preparing to go on the final phase of their journey to the source of the River Ganges, which is in the snowy reaches of the Himalayas. There can be considerable hardship and penance involved in going on a pilgrimage like this.

The Fire Puja at Hardwar. This spectacular puja is performed for pilgrims at festival times. Fire is one of the basic elements of life, and is always used in puja. The fire god Agni was important in Vedic times, and because fire is both life-giving and life-destroying, it is considered to be a god in itself.

Hardwar is famous for the Kumbha Mela, which takes place here every twelve years. It is in the Guinness book of records as the largest gathering in the world as more than 30 million attend. The photograph on page 83 shows pilgrims bathing during Kumbha Mela.

Some pilgrimage places are on the sea. The most famous is Dwarka, on the extreme tip of the state of Gujarat. This was seen as Krishna's capital city and celebrations of his birth and death take place here.

Coromin is on the southern tip of India and Rameshwaram is between India and Sri Lanka. This is famous because it is believed that Rama, Sita and Hanuman established two shrines to Shiva here. There are thirty-two wells here – one for each particular kind of sin.

Other pilgrimage sites are mountains. Kailasha (also known as Mount Meru) is high up in the Himalayan range. It is a very beautiful place and near to the sources of four of India's most sacred rivers.

Other sacred places are associated with particular deities, so Hindus will be attracted to those belonging to their own particular Ishta-devata. Shaivaite Hindus will visit Varanasi,

and Vaishnavite Hindus will visit Vrindaban where it is believed that Krishna played on the banks of the river Jumna. The city of Ayodhya is the birthplace of Rama and Mathura the birthplace of Krishna

Vrindaban, on the banks of the Jamuna, is believed to be the place where Krishna spent his childhood and youth - where he played with the gopis (cowgirls) and saved the villages from disaster. Devotees of Krishna are filled with joy when they see this place.

This is a Hindu shrine and temple at the Galta Gorge to the east of Jaipur. According to legend, Krishna passed through the Galta Gorge after escaping from attacking hordes of evil forces. These pilgrims are floating their offerings of flowers and lamps on the water.

Other pilgrimage sites are based around important temples such as the Mother Goddess temple to Kali in Calcutta, and the Vishnu temple at the Badrinath 3000 feet up in the Himalayas.

Activities

Key Elements

1 Why are the cities along the River Ganges such important places of pilgrimage?

2 For what reason do Hindus go on pilgrimage?

3 Find a map of India and look up: Varanasi, Hardwar, Rishikesh, Dwarka, Vrindaban, Ayodhya and Mathura.

Think About It

4 What effect might visiting Varanasi on pilgrimage have on young Hindus? How might it influence their faith in God and their attitude towards life, their society and their culture?

5 Why do many people in different religions feel it is important to make a journey to a sacred place?

These pilgrims are being taken across the Jamuna river at Vrindaban by a wise old man who must know the river well. The crossing from one side of the river to another is seen as a symbol of leaving one life behind and starting another.

What do Hindus do on pilgrimage?

Pilgrimages are important events in a Hindu's life and they are carefully considered and planned. They are undertaken in a spirit of austerity and self denial. Pilgrims often make very long and arduous journeys to reach these sacred places, do without material comforts and live in very basic accommodation.

When they arrive at their place of pilgrimage, Hindus may do any or all of the following:

- They perform puja at the place of pilgrimage and make offerings for their departed relatives (Shraddha rites).
- They may circumambulate (walk around) the temples in a variety of ways. Sometimes they prostrate themselves while doing so. Measuring their image in a series of prostrations as they circumabulate the temple expresses this desire to do penance.
- The highlight of the pilgrimage is the darshan – viewing the image of the deity in the inner sanctum.
- They might also visit a family priest who would offer advice and a sense of continuity, as he and his forefathers may have been in touch with this family for generations.

This is the shrine at the pilgrimage site at Paithan, which is dedicated to Eknath, a Marathi poet-saint who lived here in the 17th century. In this open area, women are selling things to be used as offerings.

The shrine at Paithan. The photo on the left shows pilgrims going forward to make offerings. Notice that one of them is prostrating before the shrine. The photo on the right shows the shrine itself.

Activities

Key Elements

1 What do Hindus do on pilgrimage?

2 Why do you think Hindus are prepared to undergo such hardships to reach these places and then perform many acts of devotion and sacrifice when they stay there?

Think About It

3 'Pilgrimage is not essential to the Hindu way of life – yet it is very important to Hindus.' Do you agree with this statement about the place of pilgrimage in Hinduism? Give reasons for your view and discuss the importance of pilgrimage in Hinduism.

Assignments

1 Imagine you are a young Hindu living in Bombay going on a pilgrimage with your family to Varanasi. Keep a journal or diary of the things you see and experience during your stay there.

2 Design a poster for an Indian Tour operator advertising their range of tours to famous pilgrimage sites in India.

9

Rites of Passage

- The 16 Samskaras
- Birth and Naming Ceremonies
- The Sacred Thread Ceremony
- Marriage Rites
- Death Rites

This Hindu wedding is taking place in south west London. Notice the Hindu priests with sacred threads, the special canopy and the symbols of puja that are used.

Rites of passage are special rituals which mark a transition from one stage of life to another. These events relate to birth, becoming an adult, getting married and death and are deeply personal and emotional as well as socially important.

They are celebrated with special actions and social or public gatherings of families and communities. They are so important that the feelings and meanings attached to these experiences are given religious and spiritual expression through rituals and sacraments.

Hindus have a great variety of rites of passage which are called Samskaras. In Sanskrit samskara means 'being made fit for use': just as cooking makes food fit for eating, so going through a samskara ensures that the person is made fit for the next stage of life.

The most important of these are
- Birth and Naming Ceremonies
- The Sacred Thread Ceremony
- Marriage Rites
- Death Rites.

The Sixteen Samskaras

There are sixteen samskaras described in Hindu religious literature, representing all the important stages of human development. They are prescribed as a kind of religious duty in the ancient law books of Manu - the Dharmashastras.

Not all sixteen samskaras may be fully practised but they will be recognised in some way. They are:

1 Conception of a child (Garbhahana). This is a ceremony performed at the first menstruation of the new bride to wish for the conception and fertilisation of an embryo (garbha) and the continuation of the human race.

2/3 Special rituals performed during pregnancy, at the second or third and the sixth or eighth month, to ensure the healthy development of the baby.

4 Birth ceremony (Jatakarma).

5 Naming ceremony (Nishkramana).

6 Child's first outing, at four months old.

7 Child's first solid food (Annaprashana).

8 Child's first haircut, 1-3 years (Mundan or Choodakarma). This is seen as a purifying ceremony, removing the impurities of being born as well as the karma of a previous life.

9 Child's ears are pierced.

10 The Sacred Thread ceremony (Upanayana) is the initiation of boys from the three upper castes into the student stage of life.

11 The start of formal education (Vedarambha).

12 Graduation from studies (Samavartana).

13 Marriage (Vivaha).

14 Retirement (Vanaprastha), usually around the age of 60.

15 Withdrawing from worldly concerns and becoming a holy man (Sanyasa). Supposed to be at the age of 75 but may be earlier or later.

16 Death Rites (Antyeshti). This will also include shraddha ceremonies which pay respects to departed relatives.

Activities

Key Elements

1 What is the meaning of the following: samsara, jatakarma, mundan, upanayana, vivaha?

2 Why do you think there are sixteen samskaras in Hindu culture, when four is more usual?

Think About It

3 Why is samskara translated as sacrament rather than ritual?

4 Why do all cultures like to have a special ceremony to mark certain stages in life?

5 In what ways are:
(i) the birth of a child in a family
(ii) becoming an adult at 18
(iii) getting married
(iv) death of oneself
(v) death of a close relative
the end of one life and the beginning of another?

Birth and Naming Ceremonies

When a baby is born it is welcomed into the world with a short ceremony. In the past the priest would have washed the baby as a symbol of purification, but today the midwife or another family member may do it.

Sometimes the family priest is invited to carry out a ritual cleansing, so he will recite prayers and hymns from the scriptures and sprinkle the mother and baby with drops of water.

In some families, when the father holds the baby for the first time, he will dip a gold jewel into a mixture of ghee and honey and touch the lips of the baby with it. He asks for God's protection and whispers a prayer in its ear:

> *May God the creator of all things grant you firm wisdom.*
> *Knowledge and wisdom are the sources of power and long life.*

Between six and twelve days after the birth the naming ceremony (Namakarana) takes place. The mother may bathe for the first time after giving birth. She will be given new clothes and the house will be filled with fresh flowers. The father, who must not have shaved since the baby was born, will now remove his growth of hair, in order to emphasise the sense of removal of pollution and new life. The family priest may conduct the ritual and cast a horoscope to determine what the first letter of the name should be. Rice grains are spread on a metal

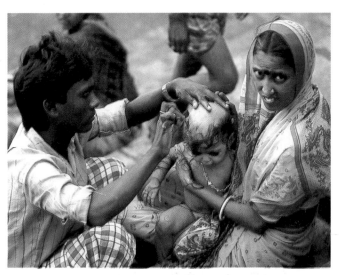

Shaving the baby's hair. This samskara is taking place in a very ordinary setting in a village in India. In England, the child might be brought to the mandir for a special ceremony.

plate which is kept in front of the couple. The father, using a gold ring or piece of gold wire, writes the name of the family deity, followed by the date of the birth of the child and the proposed name. The father whispers the name into the baby's right ear. The name has an important meaning and may be associated with gods and goddesses or with the powers of nature.

The scriptures recommend that boys' names should be of two or four syllables while girls should be of one, three or five syllables. In ancient times male names were suffixed by caste names e.g. Sharma for brahmins, Varma for kshatriyas, Gupta for vaishyas and Dasa for shudras. However in modern times such suffixes do not necessarily indicate varna or jati.

Girls names:			Boys names:		
Anvi	means	Earth	Anand	means	happy
Padma		flower	Amit		lovable
Usha		dawn	Aakash		sky
Asha		hope	Bimal		pure
Chandra		moon	Pankaj		lotus
Hetal		friendly	Vijay		victory
Hema		golden	Rajiv		lotus
Tejal		brightness	Deepak		light

Parvati, Savita, Anusuya are linked to the names of the goddesses.

Mahesh, Jagdish, Niranjan are linked to the names of the gods.

The Sacred Thread Ceremony

Most religions have special ceremonies to mark the transition to adulthood and commitment to the teachings and practice of a particular faith. In Hinduism one of the most important ceremonies for the upper three castes is the sacred thread ceremony. Members of the brahmin, kshatriya and vaishya castes are known as twice born and to enter fully into their caste they have to be initiated with the upanayana rite.

In this samskara the boy is introduced to the guru or teacher and given the sacred thread (yajnopaveet) which consists of three strands. These symbolise the three vows or promises which the young adult will have to observe and follow in his life:

1. The obligation to promote knowledge gained from all sages, thinkers and scientists (Rishi Rin)
2. The obligation to look after and respect one's parents and ancestors (Pitri Rin)
3. The obligation towards the society and nation in which one lives (Dev Rin).

It is also an initiation into the student stage (brahmacharya) and is usually undertaken for boys between the ages of eight and sixteen. It marks the boy's coming of age when he needs to understand the meaning of belonging to a Hindu community and also embark on his formal education and learning of Hindu scriptures.

In the past, the boy left home to receive his education from a guru or spiritual teacher where he would have learnt meditation and the language and teachings of the Vedas. This is not the case today, but this stage of life does require the young adult to observe celibacy and moral purity. It is a religious and a social occasion and is performed in front of family and friends.

In this ceremony the boy the boy passes from the care and authority of his mother and comes under the influence of the male members of the family. Because of changing circumstances to-day many Hindus now feel that both boys and girls should undergo this samskara.

The ceremony

The best day for the ceremony is usually chosen by the family priest or astrologer. The boy's head is shaved except for a tuft of hair on the crown.

He takes a bath and wears a special white dhoti. The boy and his mother share a special meal together, then the mother leaves the proceedings.

The boy then stands facing west opposite his father who faces east. A piece of cloth is held between father and son and songs of blessings are sung.

The priest conducts a special sacred fire ritual called homa. Offerings of rice and ghee are made to Agni the god of fire.

The boy is given new clothes and a piece of deer skin on a loop of soft cotton is placed around his neck.

Then a loop of white cotton made from three strands is placed over the boy's left shoulder, so that it hangs diagonally across his chest and under his right and is tied with a spiritual knot. The father says 'May this sacred thread destroy my ignorance, grant me long life and increase my understanding.' The boy repeats these words as he puts on the sacred thread. It is worn day and night for the rest of his life and is renewed annually at a special ceremony in September (Ganesha Chaturti, Ganesha's birthday).

The boy kneels on his right knee in front of his father or teacher and asks to be taught the Gayatri hymn, which is recited to him. The boy then takes a vow of celibacy and makes promises to obey his father, his teacher and the family priest and to concentrate on his studies. He is given a staff to enable him to follow the right path in his studies and he pretends to leave home, but is persuaded to stay for the feast and to receive presents from his family and friends.

Question
- What effect do you think the Sacred Thread Ceremony might have on a young Hindu's outlook on life and relationships with the rest of his family?

The Sacred Thread Ceremony. This is taking place in the home of a young Hindu in Crawley. Notice the objects on the shrine.

Marriage Rites

In Hinduism marriage is considered to be holy and a religious duty. It is not only the union between two partners but an alliance between two families.

In the past the partners were always chosen by the parents, but now the couple have more of a say in the matter and so marriages are 'guided' rather than 'arranged', especially in Britain.

Once the choice has been made, a priest looks up the partners' horoscopes to find a good time for the wedding. In India it would take place at the bride's home; in Britain, a hall would be booked and large numbers of relatives would be prepared to travel great distances to attend.

The wedding is often a costly affair for the bride's family, especially if it happens in her home and also because her father will probably have agreed to give a dowry to her husband. Although this is an illegal practice, it is still observed, sometimes as a matter of pride.

The ceremony

1 **The bridegroom and his family is welcomed at the bride's house.** Members of both families are introduced. The bridegroom is brought to a specially decorated altar called a 'Mandap', offered a seat and a welcoming drink, a mixture of milk, ghee, yoghurt and honey.

2 **Songs of blessings.** The bride and groom stand facing each other. A silk cloth is held between them by the priest and his assistant to form a curtain. Rice grains are distributed amongst the guests, songs of blessings are sung and the guests shower the couple with rice.

3 **The daughter is given in marriage by her father** to the groom, who puts his daugter's right hand into the hand of her future husband. Her father asks the groom to promise to be moderate in the observance of his moral duty (dharma), the earning of money (artha) and the enjoyment of good things in life (kama).

4 **Symbolic exchange of gifts.** The groom's mother gives an auspicious necklace (Mangala sootra) to the bride.

5 **The sacred fire is lit and the priest recites the sacred mantras in Sanskrit.** He invites the groom to make offerings to the fire as certain prayers are said. The bride shares in this act by touching his shoulder. To the bride he says

I am the Sun you are the Earth. May my seed, planted in you, produce children. May they outlive us. May we love and admire one another and protect each other with a kind heart. May we see, hear and live a hundred autumns.

The end of the bride's sari that hangs over her shoulder is then tied to the scarf which the husband is wearing.

6 **The taking of vows.** The husband, holding his wife's hands, says "I hold your hand in the spirit of dharma we are both husband and wife." The couple offer roasted rice to the sacred fire.

7 **The bride steps on a stone,** which symbolises a rock and her willingness and strength to overcome difficulties in pursuit of her duties.

8 **The seven steps.** This is the main part of the ceremony. The couple walk seven steps around the sacred fire reciting a prayer at each step

the first for food
the second for power
the third for prosperity
the fourth for wisdom
the fifth for children
the sixth for health
the seventh for friendship

The bride's brothers pour barley into the couple's hands, to be offered to the fire and to symbolise that they will work together for the welfare of society. The husband marks the parting of his wife's hair with red kum-kum powder for the first time. It is called soodar and is a sign of a married woman.

9 **Viewing the Pole star.** If the wedding is in the daytime, the couple will look at the sun (Surya Darshan) in order to be blessed, and if it is at night they will look in the direction of the Pole Star. The wife resolves to be unshaken and steadfast like the star.

The Pole Star is Dhruva, constant. May I be Dhruva in my husband's family.

10 **The blessings.** The couple are blessed by the elders and the priest for a long and prosperous married life.

This will be followed by a sumptuous feast to impress all the guests.

When the bride enters the house of her husband's family for the first time, she has one more ceremony to perform. She must kick over a metal pot containing wheat with her right foot so that the grain, spilt over the threshold, signifies she will bring prosperity.

The bride at a Rajasthani Wedding. Rajasthan is known for the beautifully decorated and brightly coloured clothes worn by the women. In this photo we see a young bride who has been garlanded and specially made up by her female relatives to look like a queen or goddess. Sometimes the bride wears a lot of gold jewellery which is her dowry for her husband. Since marriages are often arranged by the families, we can imagine the thoughts going through her mind on this most important day in her life.

Death Rites

In the West we tend to hide the reality of the decay of the body, but for Hindus death is accepted as an inevitable fact with the passing of time, and an opportunity for the release of the soul and the start of a new life. Although the mourners are sad, they are also glad that the person has the chance of a new life.

Cremation at Pashupatinath in Katmandu, Nepal. This is an unusual photograph which shows what really happens at a cremation. We can see how the dead body is being set alight and the whole process of reducing the body to ashes can be observed by the family.

There are various death rites which vary from region to region and family to family, although there are some common features, especially cremation.

In Indian towns and cities special cremation grounds stand ready for use and in the villages there is an area of land set aside for no other purpose. In Britain, Hindus cremate their dead at local crematoria. In India, the nearest male relative conducts the funeral rites with the help of their family and the local priest. All family members are closely involved in these last rites.

If the person who has died is a man, close male relatives bathe his body and dress him in new clothes. Female relatives do the same if the dead person is a woman.

A funeral pyre is made of wood and sandalwood , saffron musk and camphor are added to this to make it sweet smelling. This pyre may be carried to the nearest cremation ground in a kind of procession. As they approach the ground they may say

Ram's name is the name of truth. Such is the fate of all men.

The body is laid on a pile of wood then more wood piled on top of the body. Ghee is put amongst the sticks to ensure that it will burn well and act as a purifying agent. The body is placed with its feet facing south towards the realm of the god of death Yama. The son or chief mourner, instructed by the priest and other relatives, will light the pyre first at the north and then other parts. When it is alight, nuts, rice and other offerings are thrown into the flames.

After death may the sun absorb your power of sight
The breath of the winds carry your soul
May you enter the shining levels as your karma permits.
May all that is water return to the oceans
And your body return to the soil and be one with the earth.

The funeral party remains until the fire begins to subside and it is clear that the deceased body has been consumed.

After the funeral the mourners will bathe and change their clothes. Two or three days later the son comes back to the cremation ground

This is the last stage of a Hindu funeral when the ashes are floated in the river. In this photo you can see that the funeral pyre has been laid at the edge of the water to allow the remains of the body to be lowered into the water. You can see members of the family talking to the Hindu priest, who is wearing a while dhoti and is bare chested. The red cloth and garlands of flowers would have been used to cover the body in procession to the cremation ground. You can see the huge pile of funeral pyres and stretchers used to carry the bodies. It reminds you that death is commonplace.

to collect the ashes which will later be scattered on a river or kept until they can be taken to the most sacred river Ganges.

The mourning period lasts for ten days. It is not encouraged to show too much grief because it is believed that the deceased is passing on to another life and the soul is getting nearer to its final destination.

Shraddha rites are prescribed in the ancient law books. The shraddha ceremony is the annual homage paid to departed ancestors. The first one is performed at a holy place and thereafter at home. Brahmins are invited to represent those who have died, and families may commemorate all departed relatives on the same day. The brahmins are given food.

Activities

Key Elements

1 What are the main actions performed at (i) a Hindu marriage and (ii) a Hindu cremation?

2 Explain the meaning of the most important actions for those attending the ceremonies.

Think About It

1 In what way can marriage be seen as a religious duty?

2 How does this ceremony show the linking of two families as well as the union of two people?

3 Do you think the rituals for the dead help the family with their grief, or make the situation more difficult to bear?

Assignment

Find out as much as you can about the ceremonies of childhood, besides the obvious ones of birth and naming. What do Hindus do at these times to celebrate these stages?

10

Moral Issues

- The Sacredness of Life
- Suffering
- Equality and Justice

- War and Peace
- The Environment
- Wealth and Poverty

The Sacredness of Life

One of the most important aspects of religion is the extent to which religious faith and practice affects people's outlook on life, their attitude towards others, their moral behaviour and the way in which the society and culture is affected by religious rules and values. The quality of life in any society can be related to the religious life of the people.

Questions

1 Do you think religion has a strong effect on a person's moral behaviour? For what reason might a religious person try to live a good moral life? Is it possible to behave in a moral way without religious belief? For what reasons might a non religious person follow a good moral life?

2 Can you think of any examples where the religion of a country has a strong effect on people's lives? In what way is this good for society and what ways is it bad for society?

Through its scriptures and moral codes Hinduism strongly asserts the sacredness of all forms of life, in animal, plant and human realms. This is due to the belief that the universal spirit (**Brahman**) exists in every element of the universe. This is like saying that God is the source of all life and dwells in every aspect of life, so that all life is precious.

> His Being is the source of all beings, the seed of all things are that are in this life have their life. He is God hidden in all beings, their inmost soul. He lives in all things and watches all thing.
>
> Svetasvatara Upanishad.

Hindus believe that everything in the universe, both living things and inanimate matter, like rocks and mountains, is an expression of God. Living beings are connected to and dependent upon each other. In the Bhagavad Gita it says that a wise sage who has realised the truth can really see this interconnectedness:

> Thus joy supreme comes to the yogi whose heart is still, whose passions are peace, who is pure from sin, who is one with Brahman with God. He sees himself in the heart of all beings and all beings in his heart. This is the vision of the yogi of harmony a vision of which is oneness. He who sees the oneness of love, loves me in whatever he sees. Wherever this man may live, in truth this man lives in me.
>
> Bhagavad Gita 6:27-433.

The belief in rebirth means that in some way everyone is related to all living beings. Your cat may have been your brother in a previous life! Hindus also believe that all living beings are different forms of God, so they should respect all beings: rich or poor, high or low born, animal or human.

> *On a brahmin full of knowledge and good conduct,*
> *on a cow, on a dog, or on a person of unclean caste,*
> *wise men look with equal eye.*
>
> Bhagavad Gita 5, 18.

This belief in the sacredness of life and the interconnectedness of beings affects the Hindu view of:
- suffering
- equality and justice
- war and peace
- the environment
- wealth and poverty.

Suffering

Suffering of many different kinds, from the tragedy of loss of life in war and natural disasters to the mental worry about passing examinations, is an inevitable part of life.

Hindus believe in the law of karma which provides a logical explanation for suffering. All the misfortune and bad luck and tragedy is the result of actions, thoughts and deeds from the past or previous existence. If a person has performed good deeds they will have a happy life; if they have performed bad deeds they will have a life full of suffering.

This might make some Hindus fail to respond to the suffering around them because it is the person's own fault. However, many Hindus feel it is their dharma or duty to help those who suffer and the relief of suffering is a way of improving one's own karma.

There is a strong teaching of social responsibility in Hinduism. One must care for one's extended family and one's caste group. If a Hindu has servants he is expected to care for them as if they were his own family. There are countless examples of schools and colleges which are not funded by the central or state governments, but by donations from caring Hindus.

A central message of Mahatma Gandhi was the duty of a Hindu to relieve the suffering of those less fortunate than oneself. He refused to accept that the outcasts were suffering on account of their past deeds, and called them Children of God or 'Harijans'. He wrote:

> *Man's ultimate aim is the realisation of God and all*
> *his activities, social, political and religious have to*
> *be guided by the ultimate aim of the vision of God.*
> *The immediate service of all human beings becomes*
> *a necessary part of the endeavour simply because*
> *the only way to find God is to see him in his creation*
> *and to be one with it. This can only be done by*
> *service for all. I am part and parcel of the whole, and*
> *I cannot find him apart from the rest of humanity.*

There is so much suffering to be seen in everyday life in India. Millions of Hindus suffer from lack of proper medical care, shelter and nutritious food. There are numerous opportunities for the more fortunate Hindus to help their fellow humans.

One example of this is the life and work of Baba Amte. He worked with Gandhi in his youth and even lived and worked among the sweepers and scavengers to share with them the humiliation and degradation they experienced. He eventually founded a leprosy clinic in Nagpur.

The Ramakrishna mission founded by Vivekananda in 1895 was a reform movement in Hinduism which promoted social reform as well as new Hindu teachings. Vivekananda said that service to humanity was service to God. The mission encouraged the practice of karma yoga as a way of relieving suffering. This meant that service to others should be done without desire for reward, with compassion and understanding and without hurting the dignity or self-respect of the beneficiary. There are many hospitals, colleges and high schools run by the Ramakrishna mission throughout India.

The Sai Baba movement and Swami Narayan Mission have also provided schools and hospitals in India with charitable donations. The Sai Baba movement has become an international one in recent years and special schools have been set up where the aim is to

Poor people being fed at a free street kitchen in Varanasi.

enable all castes of children to live by the values of peace, non-violence, truth, right conduct and love.

The Krishna Consciousness Society (ISCON) is a form of Hinduism that has come to the West. These devotees of Krishna have set up free food kitchens for the homeless and needy within a ten mile radius of any of their temples in cities in India and Britain.

Suicide and Euthanasia

The Hindu view of life encourages a positive attitude: accepting one's gift of life and particular situation. Suicide is a denial of life and a rejection of the gift of life, so it is not accepted as a rightful act.

In the past the practice of suti (or suttee), in which a widow threw herself onto the funeral pyre of her husband, was considered to be a noble act. However this practice has now been abolished. There is also the practice of suicide as a religious act, which is mentioned in the Ramayana and Mahabharata. Mahatma Gandhi

went on a hunger strike to make his protests against injustice.

The Hindu teaching is that one has to use every opportunity in this life to achieve the goals to life and achieve a good rebirth. Committing suicide would not be an escape from misfortune, but a way of increasing misfortune in the next existence.

> *The one who commits suicide to escape the trials of life by committing suicide will suffer even more in the next life.*
>
> The Yajur Veda (40-3).

Within Hindu ethics and dharma the taking of another person's life is a great sin and a crime. Putting an end to someone's life by mercy killing is not acceptable, but is sometimes practised as it might be in any society. The whole approach to health and well being in Hinduism is based on the ancient and effective principles of Ayurvedic medicine. This kind of treatment is not based on the same principles as medicine in the West. It is a kind of alternative medicine which treats the whole person, body, mind and soul, rather than just the physical symptoms. Some of the principles of Vedic medicine which harmonise the mind and body, are now valued in western culture. Many of the illnesses of the modern world such as heart disease, cancer and ulcers are believed to be due to stress, and Ayurvedic medicine provides spiritual remedies, such as prayer and meditation, as well as natural herbal remedies to restore health.

Abortion

Abortion goes against the Hindu teaching of **ahimsa**, which means non-violence and opposition to the taking of life in any form. However, India has suffered greatly from over population and abortion is widely used a method of birth control. The Hindu view is that life starts at the time of conception, so abortion does involve the taking of life and this wrong doing will bring its own inevitable consequences. However, compassion and understanding for this moral dilemma is expressed in some Hindu scriptures:

"When a person causes an abortion in pregnancy by striking, by medicine, or by annoyance, the highest, middle and lesser punishments shall be imposed respectively."

Another text states that it is better to preserve the life of the mother rather than the foetus.

Questions

- How does belief in an eternal soul affect the Hindu attitude to suffering, suicide and abortion?

Equality and Justice

Since Hindus believe that the divine element is in everyone, although human beings might look outwardly different, inwardly they are all the same. Therefore it is wrong to discriminate against anyone or to show hatred on the grounds of race or colour. Attitudes of superiority and prejudice are based in selfishness, pride and greed which are against the central teachings of Hinduism. The ideal of selfless service to others is the ideal to follow. Mahatma Gandhi campaigned vigorously in South Africa for 20 years against apartheid.

Historically, Hinduism has a reputation for tolerance and welcoming of other non-Hindu religious minorities. There have been communities of Jews, Christians and Zoroastrians (Parsis from Iran) who have lived peacefully in India for many centuries.

The largest minority in India today are Muslims and although they have co-existed peacefully in the villages since the sixteenth century, in modern times there has been tension between Hindus and Muslims.

It might appear that the caste system does not grant equality to all Hindus, especially with regard to the outcastes or untouchables. Gandhi highlighted their plight and campaigned for their change of status. Dr Ambedkar, the lawyer who become the writer of the Indian Constitution for Indian independence in 1949, was a famous man from the untouchable caste. In 1950 the practice of untouchability was abolished and many laws have been passed since then giving special rights and privileges to untouchables to prevent discrimination. It is not acceptable to call this caste 'untouchable', it is better to refer to them as 'dalits' which means 'oppressed.' It is an offence to impose disabilities on the ground of untouchability in matters such as access to temples, public transport, education and water supplies. The law reserves a percentage of places for untouchables in schools, colleges and jobs in the public sector. This has improved their social and economic position, but has also increased resentment towards them.

Even though many Hindus are strongly opposed to untouchability, there is still some prejudice against this caste. This is because of a belief in ritual pollution. There are many tasks which bring people into contact with unhygienic substances which are considered polluting, and which in the past may have been associated with disease or death. So physical contact with dead animals, blood, excrement or any kind of dirt was considered unclean. If a person worked with such things then this pollution was permanently attached to them, so being touched by such workers would also spread the pollution to oneself. These kind of fears are behind the dislike of equality for dalits. In a survey of villages, some untouchables were not allowed to use the same well as the other castes and they were barred from entering the local temple. They still live on the edge of society in extreme poverty, doing menial tasks, but there are organisations in India today campaigning for equal rights for dalits.

The Role of Women in Indian Society

The role of a woman as a mother has always been given very high status in Hinduism. The first value a child learns is respect for their mother and in this way adoration of the mother is like the worship of God. Everything good, blissful, protective and evil-destroying is associated with a mother image. The concept of mother worship is very much part of the Hindu mentality, as the mother is the first teacher of the child.

However, in any society there are different attitudes and opinions about the role that women should play. Some Hindus in India uphold very traditional values about women and family life; others are more liberal and open-minded. Consequently the role of women as homemakers and mothers and subject to the authority of her husband is commonly accepted as is the notion of equality for men and women.

Other aspects of the Hindu way of life give men greater importance than women:
• only men may act as priests
• only sons can perform funeral rites
• only boys receive a sacred thread.

However, attitudes towards women have changed in the past 50 years and now it is possible for women to have equal social status and success as men. Indira Gandhi, for example, was a very strong, courageous and highly respected Prime Minister. After independence, women were given equality before the law and equal voting rights.

Widowhood

In traditional Hinduism a woman can only have one husband in her present life time whereas men are allowed to remarry. Since many women were married at a young age to older men they were often widowed while they were still young women in their thirties. This was seen as a miserable fate because a widow remains entirely dependent upon her husband's family and is expected to lead an ascetic life wearing plain clothes and no adornments , keeping apart from the pleasures and enjoyment of life.

In the past young widows from high caste families burned themselves on their husband's funeral pyres. Ram Mohun Roy as religious reformer campaigned strongly against this

Some social reformers in India set up educational foundations for the education of widows. This is Professor Joglekar of the Women's University of Bombay, which is a flourishing institution providing a range of qualifications for women who are actively involved in many projects to improve the social and economic conditions throughout India. The motto of this university is 'An enlightened woman is a source of infinite power'.

practice and it was abolished by law in 1829. Widows had been forbidden to remarry by law and although the 'Hindu Widow's Remarriage Act' removed the religious prohibition, attitudes did not change until 1950s. Until then widows had no education, money or social standing. Sometimes this forced them to remain unpaid housemaids in their husband's families.

Women as wives and mothers

The more traditional view of the role of women is conveyed in this passage from the Laws of Manu:

> *Where women are respected, there lives God. If the wife is obedient to the husband, and the husband loves his wife; if the children obey the parents, and guests are entertained; if family duties are performed, and gifts are given to the needy, then there is Heaven and nowhere else.*

Just as, in the Hindu concept of God, male and female aspects depend on each other, so the wife is indispensable to her husband. She is his companion, sharing his joys and sorrows and assisting him in every way. In the home the woman is likened to the various goddesses. If she is like Lakshmi, she will bring peace, harmony and prosperity to the household; if like Saraswati, she will give knowledge, education and wisdom to her children. As Rama's wife, the goddess Sita is a role model for Hindu women; she was faithful and willing to undergo great hardship for her husband's sake.

All Hindu women will expect to get married. This important stage in her life is seen as the fulfilment of her womanhood. The marriage is a holy ceremony and the woman takes vows of service, devotion and undying fidelity to her husband. She is expected to honour and respect her husband and on his death never insult his name. Breaking the marriage vows through any kind of unfaithfulness, would be socially unacceptable. Indian law permits divorce, but there are strong community pressures against it. A divorced woman usually returns to her parents or her brother and, if possible, a second marriage is arranged for her.

It is the women of the household who organise and perform daily puja. The position of a Hindu woman in her husband's family is made secure when she becomes pregnant, and especially if she bears male children. Only then does she become a full family member. Also, it is the tradition for the sons to look after their mother in her old age, so with the birth of a son her future is secured.

Having a large family is a mark of prestige, especially if there are sons. Girls are less popular since they cannot continue a family business, but are destined to marry and serve their husband's family. Thus the birth of a girl child is greeted with less joy in some families. As well as being a source of worry during their adolescence, girls are expensive as the father has to provide a dowry for his daughter, which is given to her husband as part of the marriage arrangements. The larger the dowry the more attractive she is. This has now been prohibited by law, but it remains a common practice.

> ### Questions
> - What are the similarities and differences between the Hindu and the western attitude to the role of women in the home and in society?

War and Peace

The concepts of **ahimsa** (non-violence) and **satya** (truthfulness) are the most basic and important moral principles for all Hindus regardless of their caste or stage in life.

The concept of ahimsa is therefore a central idea in the Hindu attitude towards war and peace. Ahimsa involves avoiding harming other living beings through thoughts, words or deeds. This doctrine has a long history in Hinduism and references to it can be found in the Upanishads where the virtues of 'asceticism, generosity, uprightness, non-violence and speaking the truth' are mentioned.

Hinduism has been famous for this principle of non-violence. For centuries the ideal of peaceful life in harmony with nature has been the goal of the householder's life, rather than social values based on military strength and conquest. One writer has suggested that the reason why the Indian subcontinent was invaded throughout its history is that the Hindu kingdoms did not have a tradition of military fighting and so were easy prey to invaders.

The Hindu attitude to war

In the Mahabharata the Hindu attitude to war and peace is expressed in many of the stories. The most famous of these is the Arjuna's dilemma in the Bhagavad Gita. He is faced with the prospect of going into battle against his kinsmen, his cousins and teachers. He is appalled at the thought of the slaughter that will follow. However, Krishna gives him the advice that it is necessary sometimes to fight a just war to overcome evil forces which rise up in society.

Krishna tells Arjuna that to fight for justice and truth is to fulfil the law of god. He makes three points:

- Firstly, as a prince and soldier, he has to fight for the good of his people.
- Secondly, he can only cause the death of men's bodies, he cannot hurt their souls.
- Thirdly, he is not fighting for personal gain, but for the benefit of mankind.

He must therefore fight to the best of his ability without hatred or bitterness. This approach is an example of karma yoga:

> *Think of thy duty and do not hesitate. There is no greater good for a warrior than to fight in a just war. There is a war which opens the doors of heaven. Arjuna! Happy the warrior whose fate it is to fight such a war.*

However, the mental and spiritual approach to war is as important as the deed itself, according to Krishna:

> *Prepare for war with peace in thy soul. Be in peace in pleasure and in pain in gain and loss in victory and defeat. In this kind of peace there is no sin.*
> *Bhagavad Gita 2: 31, 33.*

The Bhagavad Gita highlights the conflict between ahimsa and the duty or dharma of the warrior, and offers the solution that fulfilment of duty for the right motive and reason, especially if it is just war, is the right action to take. It also suggests that these Hindu teachings about war and peace can lead to a deeper understanding and appreciation of the nature of life and death.

The Law Books of Manu provide guidelines for right conduct in relation to war and peace. Here it states that a kshatriya should be always prepared to fight in a just war and to behave honourably. He should not kill anyone who has surrendered, or joined his hands and asked for mercy, who is asleep or disarmed, or an onlooker not involved in battle, an enemy who is wounded, or women and children. The Rig Veda also states that he must not attack the sick, the old, a child, or a woman, or from behind. These are sinful acts and lead to hell even if the warrior is the winner (Rig Veda 6-75-15).

Hinduism and Pacifism

Mahatma Gandhi is one of the most famous people in the world for his belief and practice of non-violence and pacifism as a way of fighting a war against injustice. He was greatly inspired by the Bhagavad Gita, and has been regarded as the greatest karma yogi of all time. Rather than engage in warfare, he argued that the real battle was to be fought within people's hearts.

At one time Gandhi led the movement for independence from British rule in India, but argued that Hindus should not take up arms against the British but should make their demands in a peaceful, non-violent way. He believed that non-violence would soften the heart of the attacker. This became a very potent weapon and was successful in winning independence from the British. Gandhi wrote:

> *The principle of ahimsa does not include any evil thought, any unjustified haste, any lies, hatred, ill-will towards anyone.*

Non-violence does not mean cowardice as he himself proved when submitting to blows from the police and imprisonment:

> *Ahimsa is not the way of the timid and cowardly .*

Questions

1 What kind of arguments for the just war can be found within the Hindu tradition?

2 How far do you agree with the Hindu attitude to war?

3 How might the teachings of the Rig Veda and the Laws of Manu be applied to modern warfare?

4 How might they be applied to the use of violence in any situation of conflict?

It is the way of the brave ready to face death. He who perished with sword in his hand is no doubt brave but he who faces death without raising his little finger is braver.

All Hindu prayers end with the word **shanti** which means 'peace'. It is said three times: once for inner peace, once for freedom from pain and illness and once for freedom from war and natural disasters.

Respect for the Environment

There is a Hindu saying 'The Earth is our mother and we are all her children', so respect and reverence for the natural world is part of Hindu thinking. The notion of ahimsa, combined with belief in rebirth and that God dwells in all life, means that harming any living being, is the same as harming one's friend or family.

Animals and plants

Reverence for animals is shown in a number of ways. A Sanskrit text says that the householder should share his food with all living beings:

A householder should regard deer, camels, donkeys, mice, snakes, birds and bees as his sons: for what difference is there between his sons and them?
(Bhagavata Purana 7, 14,9)

Particular plants and animals are regarded as sacred because of their medicinal properties or association with the deities. The tulsi (basil plant) is sacred to Vishnu, and the bilva or bel to Shiva. Devotees cultivate these plants and use their leaves in worship. The peepul, or sacred fig, was the tree under which the Buddha become enlightened.

Animals and birds such as the bull, tiger, mouse, peacock, eagle and swan are used as vehicles (vahana) for the various deities. Tigers, peacocks and elephants are protected animals in India. Monkeys are often treated as sacred animals as they are seen as relatives of Hanuman the monkey god and loyal servant of Rama. The same is true of elephants because of the god Ganesha. Snakes are often looked upon as guardians of the land they live in and villagers will offer bowls of milk to them. Nagas or large serpents are more like mythical beasts, and are seen as protective forces, often shown as many headed cobras sheltering the gods from any kind of harm. Shiva also has snakes and serpents twined around him both as protectors and as symbols of fertility.

Much of India has a village economy and tilling the soil inevitably means harming many creatures. This was recognised in earlier times and the law books of Manu provide some prayers and rituals to seek forgiveness for harming these creatures.

A householder has five slaughter houses: the hearth, the millstone, the broom, the mortar.
And the water-jar: by using these he sins.

The sacred cow

The most sacred animal to Hindus is the cow, and reverence for it is an expression of gratitude for life. The cow is a great source of nourishment and a giver of life in village India. Not only does it provide food through milk, butter and yoghurt but bullocks are essential for drawing carts and ploughs, while the dung is valued as manure and as fuel and it is also used for plastering floors.

Food has been left out for this cow: just another sign of the reverence shown to cows in Hinduism.

The bull is the animal on which Shiva rides and bulls are often dedicated to temples of Shiva as an act of piety or in fulfilment of a vow. Stories of Krishna show him milking cows and playing with them. So the cow is deeply revered by devout Hindus, and even in secular India today the killing of cows is banned in some Indian states and there are special retirement homes for elderly animals (mainly cows), called gowshalas. When the dangers of mad cow disease in England meant that thousands of cows would be slaughtered, some wealthy Hindu businessmen offered to have some of them shipped over to India to be looked after in one of these homes.

Vegetarianism

The main reasons for not eating beef are religious ones and it is a clear sign of religious purity and caste status not to eat any kind of meat. But there many other good reasons given today, especially by devotees of Krishna Consciousness:

- Meat eating is unhealthy because it may contain preservatives and poisons.
- Meat arouses the passions of anger and sex. The breath which utters the sacred mantras from the Vedas should not be contaminated.
- A devotee will only eat food that has been first offered to Krishna, and in the Gita Krishna only eats fruit and vegetables.
- It is much better use of natural resources and helps to preserve the environment if people have a vegetable diet rather than cultivating pasture for animals.
- If we needlessly kill animals we will have to be slaughtered and eaten in our next lives.

Not all Hindus are vegetarian, some eat mutton and chicken. Sometimes red foods such as beetroot, carrots, red water melon and red wine are not eaten because red is the colour of blood.

Fasting

Many Hindus take vows to abstain periodically from meat or other foods. Some do so on particular days of the week or lunar month. Sometimes Hindus fast for religious and health reasons. This is done in honour of the gods and is thought to bring religious merit and to improve self control and physical well being. Fasting is often undertaken by women for the benefit of their husbands or families.

Conservation of the environment

Hindus regard the whole universe as a manifestation of God. The hymn to Purusha (the creator of the universe) says:

Purusha is the whole universe, that which was and which shall be. Such is his greatness...
One quarter of all beings make up a quarter of him
The other three quarters are immortal in heaven
Thence in all directions he spreads into living beings and inanimate matter.

(Rig Veda X. 90)

The care and protection of the environment is regarded as a religious duty in Hinduism and the well-being of all mankind is seen as dependent upon proper and careful use of natural resources.

There have been several movements in recent years, led by Hindus, to campaign for and undertake projects to preserve and protect the natural environment. Two movements have been founded by Sunderlal Bahuguna, one of which is to stop the construction of a dam at Tehri which will devastate large areas of farming land, and the other is the Chipko movement which aims to prevent further deforestation of the dense forests in the Himalayas. The Chipko movement uses a form of non-violent struggle as people link hands around trees to prevent them being felled. The movement looks back to an incident in 1730 when tribal women in Rajasthan embraced trees to prevent them being felled for fuel by the Maharaja of Jodhpur. The women lost their lives as they were cut down with the trees. Their prayer was:

You guard us, you feed us, you give us the breath of life. Tree, Give me your strength to protect you.

Wealth and Poverty

One of the four aims in life is **artha** which is the gaining of wealth by honest means. Hindu law encourages Hindus to earn money so that, for example, a man can provide for his wife, children and extended family.

Guidelines on artha were given in the Artha Shastras, written by a sage called Kautilya who lived in 300 BCE. This scripture includes teachings about accounts, coinage, trade, commerce, the armed forces, weights and measures, agriculture, law, government and administration.

By the standards of the affluent western world, there is a great deal of poverty in India. There are many reasons for this. It is clearly admitted by many economists that the present day problems of India are caused by the exploitation of India's resources by the European powers during their time of colonial expansion. Also, there has been a growth in population without sufficient food production. Thus there are some moral issues associated with wealth and poverty.

The Hindu scriptures have laid down that a man may keep for himself what he needs but he should not hoard more than he needs and so deny others what they truly need.

One may amass wealth with hundreds of hands but one should also distribute it with thousands of hands.
If someone keeps all that he accumulates for himself and does not give it to others, the hoarded wealth will eventually prove to be the cause of ruin.
(Rig Veda 10-177-6)

Vinoba Bhave, a follower of Gandhi, wanted land to be redistributed from the wealthiest to the poorest as a means of overcoming poverty. He did not oppose the secular law which allowed ownership of the land but worked to persuade people to give some of their land away voluntarily. Starting in 1948, his Bhoodan movement has organised the redistribution of four million acres of land.

There are many projects underway in India to reduce poverty. Many educational and commercial projects and rural development programmes are financed by charities rather than by the government.

Activities

Key Elements

1 What is the Hindu teaching about vegetarianism, use of wealth and respect for the environment?

2 Do you think it is easy or difficult for Hindus to follow these teachings? Give reasons for your answer.

Think About It

3 Imagine a dialogue between two people about to go on active service in a modern war. One of them is a Hindu, using the same arguments as Krishna in the Gita.

The other is a soldier with no particular religious faith but who is troubled about killing. How would each of them justify the fighting that is about to happen?

Assignment

• Vivekananda, a great Hindu teacher, said at the beginning of the 20th century that the West must learn from India its spirituality, and that India must learn from the West how to improve material conditions for its people. What does this mean, and do you agree?

Word List

ahimsa   Non-harming; non-injury; non-violence; respect for life.

arta (artha) Literally 'goal, advantage or wealth'; it refers to success in worldly pursuits.

arti   The offering of light during puja, using a special arti lamp, which has five wicks in it. It is waved over the murtis and then the devotee places their hands over the light and then over their heads in the arti ceremony.

ashram   A stopping place; a centre for study and meditation.

ashrama   A stage in life.

atman   The inner self; the spiritual element, indestructible, eternal and perfect, dwelling in each living being.

avatar   Literally 'descent'; the earthly form of a deity. It usually refers to the nine avatars of Vishnu.

bhajan   A song of praise.

bhakti yoga   The path of loving devotion as a means of reaching moksha.

bhakti   Devotion in love and adoration to a chosen deity.

Brahma   The creator god – part of the Trimurti (with Vishnu and Shiva).

brahmacharya   The first stage in life, in which a young person vows to study the Vedas and to remain celibate.

Brahman   The One Supreme, all pervading Spirit; the impersonal absolute which is seen as the origin and support of the universe.

brahmin   The highest of the four castes or varnas; the priestly caste, responsible for performing religious rituals on account of their purity and tradition of learning the scriptures.

darshan   Literally 'viewing'; in religious practice it refers to paying respect and homage to a holy image, person or place, and receiving a blessing in return.

Dharma   Literally 'to uphold'; the right conduct and laws which uphold order and harmony in society.

Dharmashastras The laws and regulations which ensure that order is maintained. They include the law books of Manu.

garbha-griha Literally 'womb house'; the inner sanctum of a Hindu temple containing the images of the deity.

grihasta   The second stage of Hindu life, when the duties of marriage, family life and contributing to the welfare of society are taken on.

guru   A spiritual teacher, believed to show the way to liberations or moksha.

harijan   Literally 'children of God'; the name given by Gandhi to the untouchable caste.

havan   The part of Hindu worship which involves making offerings or sacrifices to the sacred fire.

jati   The occupation traditionally followed by a family.

jnana-yoga The path of knowledge and meditation, leading to moksha.

kama   The third of the four aims in life; the enjoyment of the senses, including erotic love.

karma   Literally 'action'; refers to the law of cause and effect - every action has its consequences.

karma-yoga The path of good deeds performed with an attitude of selflessness.

kshatriya   The second of the four varnas; the ruling or warrior class.

lingum   The symbol of the regenerative powers of Shiva, the god of destruction and re-creation.

mandir   A Hindu temple.

mantra   A short prayer or text which is repeated to focus the mind on God.

moksha The final release and liberation of the inner self or atman.

mudra A hand gesture used in Indian dance and used in some images to convey a message, such as a blessing or protection.

Mundan The head-shaving ceremony, one of the sixteen samskaras.

murti A form or image of a deity, used to focus attention for worship.

nagas Mythological snakes, seen as protectors of the gods.

OM The sacred syllable, representing the life-giving power of Brahman.

prana pratishta The literal meaning of prana is 'breath'. Prana pratishta therefore means breathing life-giving energy into an image of the deity.

prashad Sacred food; offered and then distributed to devotees after puja.

puja Paying respect to a deity as an honoured guest in the home or temple.

Puranas Part of the Hindu scriptures, largely composed of mythological stories.

raja-yoga The highest form of yoga, involving mind, body, senses and soul.

rajas Passions and ambitions; one of the three gunas.

rangoli Special patterns made from coloured powders and displayed on the ground on special occasions.

rishi A spiritually wise person.

Rta The word in the early Vedas meaning 'order' or 'fixed rule'.

sadhu An Indian holy man.

samkhya-yoga A school of philosophy which describes human nature as being made of purusha (spirit) and prakriti (matter) with the three gunas: sattva (goodness), rajas (passions) and tamas (darkness).

samsara The ever-changing world and cycle of life; the continuous process of birth, death and rebirth.

samskaras Special rituals which bring into being or mark a new stage in life.

Sanatana Dharma Literally 'The Eternal Law'.

sattva Goodness; the ability to sustain and nourish; one of the three gunas.

shakti Energy or power - especially in relation to the feminine nature and deities.

shikhara A tower or dome on a mandir, standing above the inner sanctum containing the murtis.

shraddha Ceremony in which the blessed food is offered in memory of departed ancestors.

shruti Teachings or truths which are heard or directly revealed.

shudra The fourth and lowest caste.

smriti Teachings which are memorised.

sunnyasin The fourth stage in life, in which a person renounces or leaves behind all worldly concerns and concentrates on the spiritual life.

Upanayana The sacred thread ceremony; one of the sixteen samskaras.

Upanishads The final book of the Vedas. It literally means 'sit down near by', which suggests that its teachings were only for those who sought them and listened carefully as they were whispered by their guru.

vaishya The third of the four castes: merchants and businessmen.

varna Literally 'colour'; refers to the castes.

varnaprastha The third stage in life, in which people may retire.

varnashramadharma The rules and laws which govern the duties of one's particular caste and stage of life.

Vedanta A form of Hindu philosophy.

Vedas Literally 'knowledge'; refers to the sacred books of the Hindus.

vivaha Marriage.

yajna Hindu rituals including an aspect of sacrifice.

Yajur Veda One of the four Vedas, dealing with rituals.

yatra Pilgrimage.

yoga Literally 'union'; refers to the union of the soul with God. It refers also to the way, path or method through which this union can be achieved.

yogi A person who has developed great skill and success in one of the yogas and is able to guide others in yoga.

Index